PARIS, ETC.

PARIS, ETC.

Writing and Illustrations

EDITED BY JESSIE VAIL AUFIERY

Serving House Books

Paris, Etc.

ISBN: 978-0997101034

Cover: Amanda P. Finuccio at amandapfinuccio.com

Paris Illustrations: Brigitta Racz, Tubidu Graphics

Serving House Books logo by Barry Lereng Wilmont

Published by Serving House Books
Copenhagen, Denmark and Florham Park, NJ

www.servinghousebooks.com

Member of The Independent Book Publishers Association

First Serving House Books Edition 2016

To the people of Paris, past, present, future

Fluctuat nec mergitur

CONTENTS

Poésie

Nouvelles

Essais

EDITOR'S INTRODUCTION

Paris's most recognizable symbol has inspired over thirty similar structures around the globe, but just as there is only one true Eiffel Tower, there can only be one Paris. The work in this anthology explores what The City of Light means to the French, to expats and visitors, and to those for whom *travel* is limited to an exploration of Expedia.com.

My first trip to *la capitale* was in 1984 when my mother was completing a year of medical school in Lille. Some of our new friends, a French host family, had invited us to their oldest daughter's wedding in Paris. Mom didn't have a car and couldn't afford train fare, but she had somehow persuaded a local Chinese grocer to let us hitch a ride. The truck was transporting crated vegetables like eggplant and bok choy and pungent skunk cabbage, along with a dozen or so lacquered ducks, which dangled from hooks above our heads.

The host family had a son my age, Antoine, who was also a fourth grader at the catholic school I was attending, and with whom I spent great swaths of time. The two snapshots I've managed to retain show us squashed into an armchair watching French-dubbed animé, and him kissing my cheek while I grin and feign escape. (Our activities often devolved into amorous chases: He was rather like a ten-year-old Pepé Le Pew.) At the wedding reception, I remember hitting the dance floor to David Bowie's *Let's Dance*, and then fleeing a few bars into Lionel Richie's *You Are*. Later, we ferreted flutes of Veuve Clicquot into a closet to drink and spy on guests, which resulted in the two of us nodding off like Hansel and Gretel with the party still in full swing outside.

I tracked Antoine down years later, when I returned to Paris as a student. He had an apartment in Place Clichy, and we would meet up at museums or inexpensive restaurants and engage in long conversations about the history of Paris, religion, Belgian beer—all subjects he was well versed in. He was shorter than I thought he'd be, and annoyed me one day by disclosing that my haircut reminded him more of Caesar than Jean Seberg. Still, I appreciated the fact that we could talk about anything, despite his relative traditionalism. Then I met someone—the man I would later marry—and my friendship with Antoine drifted. Years later I discovered, through social media, that he had become a priest. (I admit it's easier to picture him giving chase than leading mass.) I returned to New York to get my degree, and eventually moved with my husband back to Paris, where we stayed until 2012.

Paris was, and in some ways still is, home. My husband's family and many of our friends are there, my children are half-French, I have French citizenship. Over a decade of my life was spent in that amazing, complex, historical city: living, raising children, working. But my first memory will always be of that frigid delivery truck with its smell of skunk cabbage, and the taste of champagne in the dark. Our stories mark us. More than the news, internet memes, or statistics—as influential as these can be—our stories make us who we are. Some of the prose collected here views Paris from a geographical remove, while some emerges from deep inside the snail. Five pieces were translated from the French (one from the Russian), and others are written in an English that yearns for all that is *Français*. These are works that are jubilant, despondent, flippant, stuck, liberated, devastated, bored, solitary, joyous, in love—that explore, in short, a wide rambling space that is not just tragedy or fantasy, but all the life that happens in between.

Bienvenue.

Poésie

Ethan Joella
PARIS

Since our Paris oath, we have delivered
two babies, put one dog and one cat
to sleep, brought one wrong dog
home from the groomers, watched four grandparents
fade. We have moved one time, gone on forty-seven planes,
replaced two kitchen floors, changed three jobs. We have broken
just one window, we have uprooted
two apple trees. We have planted a hydrangea,
four different hostas, and three boxwood. We have found
two dead mice and one mole. We have sprayed
for wasps, replaced a patio, bought five cars, one that leaked
coolant, green and startling, over the school's parking lot.
We have broken five dishes
and fourteen glasses. We have forgotten sometimes

to shower. Put two girls through preschool,
gymnastics, soccer, dance classes, art classes. We have broken
zero bones , we have had one yard sale. We have defended
two dissertations, yelled at three teachers. We have gone to
five weddings, carved sixteen pumpkins. We have had Stanley Steemer
show up five times. We have bought two punch bowls, hosted
fourteen birthday parties (Rapunzel, My Little Pony, Star Wars).
We have been the tooth fairy six times (her wispy writing
in molar-shaped notes), we have sketched the galaxies
in sidewalk chalk. We have wiped tears,
placed cool washcloths on heads, we have carried strollers

up escalators. We have run farther, stayed awake

longer, sat on the porch and watched
trees and green hills in the distance. We have
melted, we have become holy,
immaculate. If the pregnancy ten years ago
was a false alarm, we said we'd go
to Paris, wait five more years to try
again. Now I think about that city
we've never been to, how gorgeous and lonely
the lights and water would have looked at night,
how we ended up waiting years for Paris
instead. We watched the sky change
as our daughters tiptoed in sea foam, the ocean
immeasurable in front of us. We squinted for a moment,
the lowering sun behind clouds,
and when we whispered to one another,
it sounded like another more beautiful language.

Heather Lang
SHUTTER

A wheel
like moving images

bright with uncaptured
people —

the 1838 Daguerreotype
of the Boulevard du Temple

or the window,
          a seeming water
-color in the rain.

Laura McCullough
THE ELISIONIST

In French, when vowels are elided,
an orthographer's tool,
the apostrophe,
orchestrates with flourish,
but always
there's the choosing
between liaison or elision,
or both as in
J'arrive à l'hôtel pour une liason.
Don't tell my husband,
who speaks French, but prefers
the schwa as in *amuïssement.*
This is all just *amuse-bouche* —
to amuse the mouth —
or more correctly, *amuses-bouche* in the plural.
Before the hotel bed, there is the lobby,
and before the *hors d'oeuvres,*
something to excite the taste buds,
and a little wine, no? Or perhaps
you'd prefer to meet me
somewhere else, say the library,
where you can't buy anything,
where whatever you use is simply on loan.
We can always touch the books'
spines rather than each other's.
There's no telling what might happen.
No telling.

David Radavich
EVERY DAY
THE WORLD STARTS AGAIN

A shopkeeper hoists baskets
with a pole, a waiter

polishes silver teapots
wearing gloves,

a thin smoker
in high heels swings

hips by
like signposts.

Even shadows greet
the sun, work starts anew

as yeasts rise,
steam kisses grates

and lovers
recover their skin

like saints
following prayer.

Food will again
enter bodies,

breaths
will gather air

the way
gases swirled

before astronomy
ached in the aerosphere.

David Radavich
WOLFE IN PARIS

How many rues he pursued —
escape and watch, exile and return —

chasing language and vocation,
museums and brothels,
cathedrals, cafés

across the Seine
and up Montmartre,

looking out
from St. Germain

toward history
and art —

for what unity,
what overall purpose?

To seize the last
pluie, soleil, ou terre,
tree and mountain,
steeple or statue,
erstwhile companion

sailing home

with pages and pages
that became impossible

and wonderful

in a suitcase that opened
and opened

and never arrived ...

Lauren Rusk
Adrift at Notre Dame

1.

The organ resounds within   this hollow mountain,
chaos rolls forth,
                            the hand of creation
works upon the darkness,
                                    rumbling my chest,
the instrument's   instrument.

Here so soon after
                            enfolding silence,
familiar though Parisian,
                                    the Quaker meeting
where I dozed, then   flailed awake

to noon to stumble
                            into all this ...
                                              folderol,
I would have said.

2.

French burbles from the pulpit,
                                    easy to ignore
when you get only scraps,
                                    except *"Le Seigneur"*...

But I didn't come to cavil
                            at *les masculins et féminins,*

rather, to feel
                    what I can.

3.

The priest looks kindly
                    in my direction
as though at a grandchild.
                                        I hear
"*vous imaginez*"…
                              "*mystère*" …
"*aimer*," to love;
                    why not

give up this problem of belief?
                                        Just feel —

but through the senses   there's the rub.

For me, the spirit stirs
                    in the trees,
in a painting,
                    in a face —

an old Quaker woman's
                    furrowed peace.

Maybe even here —
                    the glass-struck light,
these greens and blues,

        gold and scarlet fashioned into …

Now he's angry.
                    The finger jabs:

"*impératifs du papa.*"

But then, "*Enfin,*"
                    the congregants turn
and give one another
                    "*la paix,*"
the handshake,
                    touch
what is, what is not.

4.

Around the vast perimeter,
altars, alcoves — one unlit,
a jumble of storage
we're supposed to glide by.

A single stone tenant
reclines on a dais
as they seem often to do.
Some understanding has come to him.

He lifts a gentle hand to tell it
          to the chairs,
     the scaffolding and coils of wire,
the foolish bubble wrap
                    foaming from its box,
the vacuum machine …

5.

A donkey pokes his nose out
from a frieze called Le *mystère*
de l'humanité du Christ.
Providing the flight from Egypt,

he gazes at me abstractedly,
ears pricked as if he hears —
what? and wonders why he's there.
Among many gospel figures
the donkey stands out, his head
the highest relief.
I love
his obscurity,
the way he loiters
in the now,
his sensitive muzzle
inviting — though it's not permitted —
touch.

Wendy Barnes
The FLÂNEUSE,
OR WOMAN PENDUE

The Hôtel des Grands Hommes
is her intended

point of departure.
In the salon, the *flâneuse*

straightens her *cravatte*,
fingers her walking stick,

winds her pocket watch,
regards the passing cars

out on the *Place du P___*.
In the corner

tiny Frenchmen exchange
elaborate salutations.

Her mind alights into the teeth
of the night, in order to,

perhaps, *cherche la femme*,
proclaim upon the *physiognomie*

of a *peuple, Paris à table,*
Paris dans l'eau,

through the *boulevardes*
end to end veining the Paris

of chimera that drips its past
and present light

upon the *passants*,
the meaty *fleuve.*

Her heart or heart
de femme beats

to break
across the casement.

She adjusts one chartreuse glove,
regards the musty relics

of the gilded, gallic ages,
delicate *objets* and masks,

a photo of a *colonel*
in black and white *Indochine*,

flanked by bare-chested natives,
his foot atop a tiger

freshly slain.
The bell at Saint Sulpice

strikes twelve in Paris
and elsewhere,

say Ft. Lauderdale, TVs
blare the local news,

sunset gnashes over lawns,
and the wives

serve dinners, stifling
coughs and sniffles

like they surely must
across the world.

The *flâneuse*, phony revenant,
ranges round

the boundaries of the battle
suspended, hung or hanged

like Foucault's pendulum,
perpetually oscillating

in the Pantheon,
measuring the earth's rotation.

Wendy Barnes
MEN TO RUIN, MEN TO DEATH

Knowing both the danger
of the game and the price
of plain surrender, Salomes
watch the earth regenerate
on rumor, blood, sea water,
wine, and bone. The name
can mean both razor-spiked
and sponge cake-lined
seduction, spit and gravitas,
a name coincident or not.
A Salome lingers, odor of orange
blossoms and rancid meat, interpreted
from everywhere. The image — just
the cliché outline of her gestures,
burlesque princess spoiling for more.

We mark her steps, as she leads
some young man or other by his mind
along the ice-encrusted shore.
See here, my dear, he falters.
She balks. One black-sheathed foot
hovers underneath her petticoats (black
like widowhood, like city soot) till
she decides — according to her reputation —
and plants the shoe into the snow.

Is that her fleeing to the coast
of Galilee or Baltic Sea? Far
from where the cows or camels
low and mothers churn their bitter
milk, lies the crusty lip of ocean,
her imagination's brink, where currents
wash the daily poisons out to sea.
Or, is she not the stripper built of carnage,
but a creature as authentic as a photo?
Does she stand quite frozen, corseted,
dark hair restrained, one hand resting
upon a gilded chair? Far beneath her
window and regard, in the cobbled street,
another veiled figure lets one fall.

Kathleen Graber
ANNIVERSARY

On Jan. 5, 2005, NASA noted a milestone:
10,000 days since Voyager 2's launch.

This morning Neptune arrives through my computer:
the most beautiful image
in the Solar System, you write, romanticizing, just a bit,

your attachment. The drama of the deeply non-human is so slow
it escapes me. Taken by Voyager 2 in 1989, the planet captured today

would look the same: a swirling giant —
  blue methane gas, clouds
& its own persistent storm, The Great Dark Spot, shaped like the red bruise

in Jupiter's sky. The descendent of the augurer & haruspex
is how Benjamin described the photographer. *The scene of a crime,*

he said, of Atget's eight thousand heavy 7X9-inch glass plates.
But doesn't any snapshot stop a thing dead?
  I'm traveling.

The hotel is almost empty: Saturday, just off a highway of corporate parks.
In the lot, an abandoned gray van, its windshield smashed, rests oddly

across the tidy lines. Can we imagine
missing this? Wanting a photograph
to document that cluster of garden apartments behind two rows of stunted pines?

What's more embarrassing than loving
  the obvious? What if you'd sent me
Venus or Saturn's rings? Atget, too, wants for obscurity. But I can't stop
looking

at the reflections in the door-glass & shop windows: bare branches &
white sky
above the slender samovar, a shelf of bottles & the flowerpots
                                                                inside,

& Atget himself, the thin legs of his awkward tripod & the anachronism
of the camera's drape — even then — inserting itself between and
over

the two blurred faces — they've been moving! —
  looking out. Later, you write:
To understand blues, you must understand breathing. And I suddenly see you,

slightly drunk, unearthing the old vinyl, turning up the volume, pleased,
    for now,
to be completely alone. When you insist that Duane Allman's
    improvised solo —

In *Memory of Elizabeth Reed,* live at the Fillmore East — depends on
varying the *room* between notes,
                        I think you must be talking about *timing.*

Is the edge of the galaxy any more remote than this street in 1908: dark cafes,
a drum, an iron deer, a baby Bacchus, hung up above the signs? Given a century,

wouldn't we reach it? Atget's head has been lost in the glass's confusion —
mirror & membrane — swallowed up in the round gaze of the woman —

is it a woman ? — on the right.
                        Voyager, its pockets full of old *hellos,* is slipping off

into interstellar-space.
                    In the end, it's still a matter of distance, how far

we will go to bring something back. Neptune & its eight cold moons
are four & a half thousand kilometers from the Sun.

Beneath its atmosphere, it has —— like the second, split open & emptied ——
no core.
We cannot foretell the future but go on, instead, like Benjamin's angel,

predicting the past.
            Once I thought each day would be another day
for misfortune.
                The photographer would fail again to erase himself,
to become only an *eye*. But, surely, Atget means for us to find him,
means
for us to go on finding him, again & again,
                                    preserved in preserving

an almost vanished world. *I can claim to possess all of Vieux Paris,*
he wrote, offering his archive to the State.

                            ...beautiful facades, beautiful

woodwork, the door knockers, the old fountains...
                                    To inscribe ourselves
in what we love —— into ragmen & wheels, the watch & the measuring stick
——

& to be inscribed
            in turn. Is there a more perfect metaphor for this?
The black swath of his workcoat falls like a winter scarf below her chin.

Kathleen Graber
DAS PASSAGEN-WERK

The first structures made of iron served transitory purposes: covered markets, railroad stations, exhibitions.
            — Walter Benjamin

On the top shelf of the closet, someone —
     the last resident, or the one before —

has stored up cards of bobby pins, coat buttons, & the thin lathe
& bakery thread of old kites.
                    But the wind remains
unboxable.
   I'm trying to be through with things, to sign on

for the invisible. The various species of small desire, perhaps, we preserve
in the dim diorama of the chest. If we know they are there at all,
they're nothing —
          taxidermy of absence
announcing that this is where what we want would be,
  if only

everything were possible.
                We are the ambitious arcade-makers
who cannot get it right: our media betray us. *Glass before its time*
& premature iron:
          an architecture of metaphor, of longing
& constraint.
   The sharp-boned corset was a cage, & emptied on the floor

beside the bed, it became a ruin, the collapsed rafters
of the waist.

    But isn't the body an arcade, too?

Not some close crawlspace or blind roof to cover what we are —
but a crystal palace,
           the warm, tactile marketplace

for all that does not last. *The most brittle and strongest*
materials. Is it a question of morals
                 to want to touch all we can?
There are words that house in their meanings the notion of the temporal:
fairground & carnival. Diversion, the crooked street where no one

belongs. What issues is always *passage:*
                   whether we think we're moving
or not. It doesn't matter what avenue we choose.
                      Four a.m.
on a dune in November, & I am here because
I said I would be. I set my clock to see the meteors extinguish
themselves

on schedule in the atmosphere above the sea.
                  I'd like to tell you
that in a year from now I'll still remember how I feel today,
but what was I thinking then on my back in the sand? There's so little
honesty in the world.
        Not all the light that falls through the girded panes

is *dirty and sad.* It's that, but it's that
                 & something more.
To clean the eaves I need the desk lamp
& the extension cord. Far back against the chimney… what?
Another suitcase,
       Some broken screens. In the dark, it's easy to believe

the earliest arcade must have seemed like heaven: transparent
interior, vaulted hall with a ceiling that disappeared. All obvious
pleasure —

    speck-swirl in shafts of sun, &...
after the stalls closed, a crinolined moon, its luminous hoop hung up
on a metal beam —

            & promise. First, the rail station,
with its small alter of happiness at the intersection of the tracks,
& the hot house, & the exhibition...
the dusty fata morgana of the winter garden.

Jeanie Greensfelder
A CHAMPS-ÉLYSÉES STROLL 1980

On a torrid day, traffic and tourists sweat
and we trudge toward Café Ladurée.
I'm determined to taste the famed macaroons
my friend raved about.

My husband sights a nearby brasserie
and wants to skip the Café Ladurée,
souring my Paris magic.
I hurl vintage hurts at him:
You don't love me. You never loved me.
His eyes flare and his lips quiver.

Then his body snakes across ten lanes of cars,
leaving me gilded in guilt, scared and stranded,
staring at the Arch of Triumph.
He had stopped smoking,
and returns, puffing a cigarette,
punishing me, hurting himself.

Two tired tourists call a truce.
We march in league down the *Champs*
toting a memory, a slice of time
toasted with heat, hot words, and smoke.

Philippe Soupault
HANDS THAT PRAY

— Translated by Gregg Ellis

In the sky magnificent smoking ships
and on earth tonight
there is a man writing
near a candle
with a fountain pen
He's thinking about grey birds
about how the grey birds are slow waltzes
He's thinking about countries he doesn't know
the way you think about your sleeping dog
He knows a lot of things that don't have names
on earth and in the skies
where splendid ships are taking off
The trees are asking for silence and rain
There's a man writing near a candle
near a sleeping dog
who is thinking about the moon
who is thinking about the Good Lord
And then there are these butterflies
little advertisements of paradise
homes of well-dressed angels
owners of elegant canes
and luxurious simple cars
Angels are friends
you ask for advice about choosing a tie
and who answer sadly
Choose the one that matches the color of your eyes

The angels disappear in the candle flames
only the trees remain
and naturally the animals we forget
they hide
Those brave ones know silence is the rule
at this hour of the courageous night
at this hour when prayers
and songs drift down on cotton ladders
This is the hour when you also see
eyes that don't want to close
motionless seraphs
Angels of Paris lend me your wings
lend me your fingers
lend me your hands
Must I still sleep such a long time
my head heavier than a sin
Must I die without a sound
in the silence the trees are asking for
near a candle
near a sleeping dog

Philippe Soupault
WESTWEGO

— Translated by Gregg Ellis

All the cities in the world
oases of our troubles dying of hunger
serve cool drinks
to the memory of loners and maniacs
and sedentaries
Cities of the continents
you are flags
stars fallen to earth
without really knowing why
and the mistresses of today's poets

I was walking one summer in London
hot footed and heavy hearted
near black walls near red walls
near long docks
where the giant policemen
are pointed like exclamation marks
You could play with the sun
that perched like a bird
on all the monuments
traveling pigeon
daily pigeon
I walked through the neighborhood called Whitechapell
pilgrimage of my childhood
where I met only
very well dressed people

sporting the latest hats
and women selling matchbooks
sporting boater caps
who yelled like French women farmers
to attract clients
penny penny penny
I went into a bar
third class locale
where Daisy Mary Poppy
were sitting next to fishermen
who chewed tobacco as they drifted off
to forget the night
the night slowly inching closer
the night and the scent of the river and the high tide
the night that tears sleep up

it was a sad day
of copper and sand
that slowly flowed among memories
deserted islands dust storms
for animals roaring with anger
who bend their heads down
like you and like me
because we are alone in this city
red and black
where all the stores are groceries
and the best people have very blue eyes

It's hot and today is Sunday
it's a sad day
the river is very unhappy
and the town people have all stayed home
I'm taking a walk near the Thames
one single boat floats along to reach the sky
the frozen sky

for today is Sunday
and the wind didn't kick up
it's noon it's five o'clock
no one longer knows where to go
a man is singing without knowing why
like I'm walking
when you're young it's for your entire life
my childhood in a cage
in this musical museum
at Madame Tussaud's
Nick Carter and his bowler hat
he's got a collection of pistols in his pocket
and a pair of handcuffs as stunning as obscenities
Near him the Knight Bayard
who looks like his brother
this is a sacred story and also the history of England
near famous criminals who no longer have names
Where did I go when I went out
there aren't any cafes
no lights that make our words take off
there aren't any tables you can lean on
to not see anything to not watch anything
there aren't any glasses
there isn't any smoke
only sidewalks long like the years
where blood stains blossom in the night
I saw in this city
so many flowers so many birds
because I was alone with my memory
near all those iron fences
that hide gardens and eyes
  on the banks of the Thames
  a beautiful February morning
  three Englishmen in short sleeves
  sang at the top of their lungs

tra la la tra la la tra la la dee da
Bus tea rooms Leicester Square
I recognize you although I've never seen you
only on post cards
my nanny received
dead leaves
Mary Daisy Poppy
little flames
in this average bar
you are the friends a 15 year old poet
tenderly admires
while thinking about Paris
along a window
a cloud passes
it's noon
near the sun
Let's walk to be silly
run to be happy
laugh to be strong

Strange traveler traveler without any baggage
I never left Paris
my memories didn't leave for a second
my memories kept following me like a little dog
I was sillier than sheep
that shine in the sky at midnight
it's very hot
I say to myself very quietly and very seriously
I'm very thirsty I'm really very thirsty
I've only got my hat
key to fields key to dreams
father of memories
didn't I ever leave Paris
but tonight I'm in this city
behind every tree streets

a memory watching for me to go by
You are my dear old Paris
but tonight at last I'm in this city
your monuments are the mile markers of my fatigue
I recognize your clouds
hanging onto chimneys
to say Adieu or Good Morning to me
night you are phosphorescent
I love you very much
all your cries are cries of tenderness for me
I'm like Aladdin in his garden
where his magic lantern was lit
I'm not looking for anything
I'm here
I'm sitting on a café terrace
and I'm openly grinning
thinking about all my famous trips
I wanted to go to New York or to Buenos Aires
to know the snow in Moscow
leave one night on a steamer
for Madagascar or Shang-hai
go up the Mississippi
I went to Barbizon
and I reread the travels of Captain Cook
I fell asleep on elastic moss
I wrote poems close to an anemone
gathering the words that hung on branches
the little train reminded me of the Trans Canadian
and tonight I'm smiling because I'm here
in front of this trembling glass
where I see the universe
laughing
on boulevards in streets
all the punks go by singing
the dry trees touch the sky

let it rain
you can walk without tiring
as far as the ocean or farther
out where the ocean is beating like a heart
closer daily tenderness
lights and barking dogs
the sky has uncovered the earth
and the world is blue
let it rain
and the world will be happy
there are also women who laugh looking at me
women whose names I don't even know
children cry out from the playgrounds in the Luxembourg Gardens
the sun has really changed in the last six months
so many things are dancing in front of me
my sleeping friends everywhere
I will see them tomorrow
Andre whose eyes are the color of a planet
Jacques Louis Theodore
tall Paul my dear tree
and Tristan whose laughter is a great peacock
you are living
I've forgotten your gestures and your true voice
but tonight I'm alone I'm Philippe Soupault
I'm slowly walking down the Boulevard Saint Michel
I'm not thinking about anything
I count the street lights I know so well
coming up on the Seine
    near the bridges of Paris
and I speak out loud
all the streets are tributaries
when you love this river where all the blood of Paris flows
and that is filthy like a filthy whore
but that is also simply the Seine
you talk to like your mother

I was very close to her
going by without regret without making any noise
her extinguished memory was an illness
I leaned on a stone wall on the quay
the way you kneel to pray
words fell like tears
sweet like candies
Hello Rimbaud how are you
Hello Lautreamont are you holding up well
I was twenty years old not a penny to my name
my father was born in Saint Malo
and my mother in Normandy
I myself was baptized in Canada
Hello me
Oriental rug dealers and beautiful women
who wander the streets at night
the ones who keep the warmth of streetlights in their eyes
those for whom pipe smoke and a glass of wine
seem a little dull
know me without knowing my name
and pass by saying Hello you
and yet there is in my chest
little suns turning around
great giant of the boulevard
tender man of the Court House
is lightening prettier in springtime
Her eyes my lightening are scissors
drivers I've still got seven bullets left
not one more not one less
not one single of them is for you
you're as ugly as cross examiners
and I read on all the walls
rugs rugs rugs and rugs
the great convoys of experience
near us near me

Swedish matches

Parisian nights have strong scents
that leave regrets and headaches
and I know it was late
and the night
the Parisian night was going to end
the way a holiday does
everything was in its place
and nobody said a word
I was waiting for the curtain to rise
the sun comes up like a flower
a dandelion
huge mechanized machines
only waiting for encouragement
start rumbling and drive off
faithfully
you no longer know whether to compare them
to ivy
or to grasshoppers
fatigue has disappeared
I see sailors leaving
to clean soot
tug boat mechanics
rolling their first cigarette
before firing up the heater
over in a harbor
a captain takes out his handkerchief
to wipe off his brow
as he often does
and myself the first one this morning
I manage to say
Good Morning
Philippe Soupault

Philippe Soupault
BELLS OF PARIS

— Translated by Gregg Ellis

Bells of Paris
have you forgotten your city's purple sky
and the loud hum you watch over ?
Bells of Paris
all the little people in your neighborhood
are impatiently awaiting your return
There's the florist on the corner
who is asked the impossible
the watchmaker who can't seem
to set the exact time
the seamstress has lost her thread
the ice cream man is scared to play his jingle
the glass maker has lost his voice

Laure-Anne Bosselaar
A PARIS BLACKBIRD

Along the Seine's left bank, near the *Pont-Neuf*, on the mansard roof
of my hotel, a scruffy blackbird squats by a chimney pot. Every day
for a week now, I have listened to him sing his April *a capella*.

Not once has he repeated the same song, not once has he left
for the chestnut trees by the river, where he would have a better chance
of being heard, a better chance of enchanting some bronze-breasted female,

or lovers taking time off from noise. His song is all that counts.
It soars over roofs and terra-cotta chimneys, its trills hushed by taxis,
cars and trucks coughing through the Parisian rush.

On the right bank of the Seine, three hours into Le Louvre's maze, past
Persian mosaics, glass-caged coins and Egyptian amulets, I slip
out of the tourist herd and head for a chair in a corner of the Greek Hall.

I sit there, exhausted, numb with knowledge and history, and stare at the bust
of an old woman, labeled *Anonymous, Greek, 11 BC*. She looks at me: weary,
terrible with banality, lips open, neck taut as if she were about to sing.

And as the crowds flock toward the *Venus de Milo*, nod at her beauty,
gawk at her perfect breasts, I look at this nameless woman — as I did
the scruffy blackbird — and listen for the cry caught in her bronze throat.

Renée Ashley

THE CRAZY DOG LADY CONSIDERS CANCELING SOME OF HER SUBSCRIPTIONS

She's got to stop reading those journals: now she's been told there's a snail: on one side of its head a folded penis somewhat like an ear & another whose member — disposable — is shed like a sigh after sex That's it for escargot & by association "Claire de Lune" & crème brûlée She's done But then a friend brings Paris gifts: a creamy leather coin purse: two small sweet chambers the dog lady thinks of as numbers 1 & 2 of the cow's quadruple stomach-hoards & a flip book — *un folioscope!* — in which a *Citroën 2 Chevaux* drives into or out of — she can't really be sure — a book left behind on a bench *C'est un bon cadeau de Paris* but that's it for her French She's never been to that country of course but it's been on her mind: an article on the catacombs A huge municipality of bones in beggary heaps in the dark beneath the *Ville-de-Lumière* Then after 1810 dry bones dealt out like cards: femur femur skull skull skull The full house of the body for building roofs & walls Those calcareous heads: accents capstones horizontal-mid-wall stripes like chair rails: *tête-à-tête-à*-cheerless-*tête* The artful stacks assure all the bones will find their home inside those narrow quarry halls Then the smaller bone-bits — vertebrae & tarsals — tossed behind the walls like trash Rare a body named or left intact But what she really wants to know & never will? The names of the souls who drew the unripe bones from their morbid fatty stews & turned that fat to soap They cleaned the bones of what was left & built more bone walls Tapped further skulls for trappings Six thousand dead & probably a thousand more All beyond the creepy lintel some man carved in stone: *Arrête! C'est ici l'empire de la mort* It's like cartoons — where's Scooby Doo? It's a Scooby treat in spades in there! But life's a grisly bit of luck no matter how you break it up And what the hell: Who comes through life unbroken? Still we have at least those two compartments as she knows: alive & dead & Yes & no & variants: come & stay then leave then come again Who'll care? She'll never go: She's claustrophobic Her feet too flat She couldn't leave her dogs that long She'll stay at home again & watch the sunset sliced like bread by trees She'll read some more She'll watch TV Pick up the poop outside & wait to see what travels to her door She knows enough not to make assumptions Has bits of oddball knowledge like: The insect-eating elephant shrew — also called a *sengi* — is actually related to the great gray thing Who could need a fact like that? But on the other hand she read just yesterday: A black bear killed a college kid not twenty miles from her house Their last bear-death? One-hundred-twenty-years ago — so who is changing? The bear & boy she thinks out loud The ozone The oceans How signals fly through air The bees are dying for some thing's sake But not her Not yet The earth still spins She does get that Its axis never plumb-line straight But it's not the place it used to be & she & it — once counting on sagacity — now pitch towards insanity

Anne Harding Woodworth
PAPILLON DI SETA BLU

I sing of him, nameless Italian
in a sleeping Paris full of moon
and fading carriages at midnight.
Elegant foreigner in tails and cufflinks,
he is luxurious promise,
the hopeful of a first verse.
And I sing it, sing and sing it because song
never browns the lapel's gardenia of a first verse.

So when he says *bonne nuit, bonne nuit,*
buonanotte to the lamps and to a cat,
I sing the first verse again,
and his farewells remain unsaid,
dapper man along the Seine,
top hat on his head.
And I sing it, sing it, sing it because
first-verse lightnesses turn back the hands of a pocket watch.

So when at dawn the top hat, tails, and gardenia
float under the bridge
and I sing the first verse again,
nothing has gone into the river, nothing cold
and violent as the city comes to life.
The stranger stands there, still, crystal cane in his hands,
bow tie of blue silk against his white vest.
And his exile goes unsung, because song
sings the way we would have it sing.

Anne Harding Woodworth
ANDRÉ KERTÉSZ, PHOTOGRAPHER

Disembodiments stalked him wherever he was.
Not the Eiffel Tower — the bridge that severed it.
Not the fork — its shadow on the table.

He couldn't go out any more, was slowing down
so he looked out his window at roofs and faded shutters
until he turned inward and became the warrior's prosthesis —

detached and splayed within a dark closet,
while naked women undulated darkly in his fun house mirrors.

Whose outsized midriff is that? Whose bulbous calf
is curving like a spoon? Whose arm within the paddles
of a kitchen fan? And where do all the bodies sing? or sleep?

At last he stayed inside for good and looked
toward warm enclosing chairs, and at the end
he laid his head against the crocheted antimacassar.

Christopher Buckley
THE ABORIGINES IN THE JARDIN DES PLANTES

Barely arrived for the last
of autumn, for that thick
daylight in stippled drifts
through a gingko's yellow fans,
for beeches going up
like the gods' lost fire —
and down the gravel promenade
the arch of tailored sycamores
vanishing to a point
in a smoldering haze.

We praised a persimmon tree,
its free-floating heaven
of auburn moons —
we praised the greenhouse,
Rousseau's equatorial palms,
the exorbitant atmosphere
sustaining the dark fronds.
Yet each day found us
before a gate to that stand
of woods, looking up to see
which of the life-sized
molds of men and women —
infused so they'd photosynthesize
and turn longingly towards the light's
blanched heart — still held

amidst the tutelage of leaves;
and which, giving up the spirit
of those breathing days, climbed on
out of themselves, no more finally
to the sky than smoke unthreaded
against the wind-sheared grey.

When only two or three still clung
by something as impenetrable
as faith, we turned and left them
where a few chartreuse sprays
still managed to pick some life
from gusts, left them with their heads
listing a little to one side —
a slow study for the absent blue —
but looking as though they might
at any moment succumb
to the river mist and drowse;
or perhaps, we silently agreed,
as if listening, as if
the thrummed stations of the air
were fully invisible with wings.

Christopher Buckley
ON THE EIFFEL TOWER

How little
does justice
to the thin air
and the height
of the cold, except
perhaps this needle
in the blue — where
before there was
no means for clouds
to abrogate their duty
for filling sky in
a beautiful way, there
is now this span of open
lattice work, spun space
to space, erasing absence
and coming to a point.

And rising
up inside
it seems knitted
with the intuition
of birds with whom you
share the view and feel
that vertiginous breeze
rifling the gold buds
of birch trees, driving
the swans like white petals
across the slate ponds below.

Wrought iron
was strung up
in the substanceless
abstraction of thought,
set somehow against all
the trips and balances
of nothing, the engineering
of the air. Above
the pylons he arched
the shrinking heavens
with girders resembling
an aviary or pergola,
then figured out
the twelve thousand pre-
fabricated parts, the 2 ½
million (more or less)
rivets in their bare
and steely sequence,
and so turned aerodynamics
around on a curve
of quadrilateral legs,
crossed-braced so precisely
that the bending
and shearing predilections
of wind were steadily
transformed to forces
of compression
so even in the hypothetical
troughs of a hurricane
there would be less
than nine inches sway.

Knowing how
an effect diminished

uniformly from a point
this master of bridges
out-wondered the changing,
free-fall rivers of the sky.
Against gravity, and with
the foregone and unbending
resistance of the cognoscenti,
he elevated the function of iron
in the world, and clearly saw
how it would accommodate this
impending and audacious grace.
Even a modest office emerged —
a nest on the final terrace
for the uncluttered atmosphere
of work, complete with wireless,
telegraph, a glass lantern on top
to clock the advanced in weather,
and also with chairs, a table,
fine glasses and Veuve Clicquot
chilling for the two times Edison
would share this rare altitude,
this bright fabric of the mind —
this, the first sound place where
you could stand back a little and
gain a degree of perspective, a place
from which you could praise, almost
objectively, the handiwork of the earth.

Christopher Buckley

PHOTOGRAPH OF MYSELF BY MODIGLIANI'S GRAVE, PERE LACHAISE, 1984

Not a breath of wind in the inarticulate trees, late
November, and by 4:00 the gauzy light above them
has already begun to fail, barely enough now
for photographs, one reason we've come to these

rococo tombs and stand about as bold as crows.
This small Babylon of hills wears away with dusk
and it takes little then to turn over the notion
of another world —— that distance, say, pearled

momentarily through the threadwork of boughs
or, out of range of this ice-blue sky, some shining
rampart beyond these skin-grey scarps —— especially
if you'd just dogged your fate and found yourself

delivered to the Costa del Sol, to drift weeks away
deep into October on a sherry-colored inlet and a bay
where shore birds skimmed the background music
of the waves, then lifted into the silk trees' gold ellipses....

We come to the austere and polished onyx of Proust,
an immoderate monument to Wilde with wings soaring
headlong for the rising night, which is overtaking
everything by the time we stop a student who can

point to Modigliani among a city block of graves
so dull, so even, they could almost be cement...
Amedeo who cherished stone, the spirit's shape unlocked in it, the soul's thick dust, is marked here

by a dirt-poor slab, his name and date worn down
while the clouds killed time, much the way the black
weight of his luck undid his lungs and let the light go
from him like bees smoked out to an unredeeming

blue, the same insubstantial air Jeanne Hebuterne
fell through a day behind his death and so shares
this unaspiring space and love at last. And we
touching these names, wish simply that whatever

flame remains will not die out of our eyes wholly
unremembered and without form. So when the photo's
snapped, I do not appear to be the visiting bon vivant
of modest ambition and comfortable luck — I'm only

somber in my Spanish coat, nonplussed in a red scarf
at my throat representing nothing more than warmth.
I am looking into the flash as if I still expect to live
forever, or as though I've at least discovered in the dark

at my back why, at 36, I've outlived his misery
and genius and can now walk ingenuously through
the world a little more unmindful of my age and old
shortcomings. And when I must take a plane back

across a winter sea, I can be consoled knowing that
no man's finally the man he would rather be. Thus
I'm flattered and pose gratefully before the dead while
these winsome stars circumscribe the night, obliquely

telling all, yet leave some room between them
for every death to come, for my abstract devotion
to clouds as if to some hope immured, as if this
unremitting sky held nothing personal against you.

Christopher Buckley
PARIS DISPATCH

> Oh lucky lucky life. Lucky life.
> — Gerald Stern

I love a place as obvious as Paris. I'm staying at the *Grand Hotel Jeanne D'Arc* for $60 a night and I know *fin de siecle* bistros with *service compris*. I have an L.L. Bean cotton sport coat the color of the leaves along the *Champs Elysees*. I'm a beige tourist like the rest, and blend in along the river walk. I'm quiet and polite with my 75 words, and everyone still in town in August is nice to me when I say *Merci Madame* the way I was taught in kindergarten from our French nuns, Madame Rose and Madame Adrianne.

I love saying *Boulevard Montparnasse, rue Monge, rue du Faubourg St-Denis*, and knowing the immediate, vibrant ligatures of the air. 4 years old and I pronounced perfectly phrases *en Français*, was awarded gold and silver stars on my school collar.

Who else but the French can pile up so many vowels, such sonorous diphthongs over coffee with milk, can offer the mellifluous directions of the boulevard, or the resplendent assonance of just ordering lunch?

Occasional clouds roll over the afternoon like *boules* the men are pitching in the parks, keeping the swelter down. Only an afterthought of rain around 5:00, just long enough to browse the only English bookstore and come out with the dust.

Almost 8 Francs to a dollar and we are eating *Chaum, Morbier* and *Reblochon* — we're drinking little cups of champagne at the neighborhood bar around the corner from our hotel. Our Metro stop is either St. Paul or Bastille — saints or revolution, this far over 40, it doesn't matter now. Still there's plenty to be said for doing nothing, for paying attention — anonymous beneath the clouds — to the aimless crunch of your shoes over centuries of decomposed granite in the *Tuileries*, over the bridge to *Ile St. Louis* or to the *Jardin des Plantes* where the dinosaurs have been updated and the flower beds appliqued with saffrons and blues, where the ancient pines and pin oaks loiter at the edges, just off *rue Lacepede* and *rue du Cardinal Lemoine*.

The first thing off the train in *Gare du Nord* I saw the sun-white domes of *Sacré-Coeur*, and took off down the wide sidewalks blessed with light, putting one happy foot in front of the other with that expansive feeling that you're going to live forever — and my mind flashed to the cover of *The Red Coal*, that black & white photo of Stern with Gilbert in 1950 — thin and serious among all the Parisians on the generous pavement. Stern, too young, of course to know what he would understand 30 years later about Pound and Williams, about fame and obscurity, about the lesson time teaches you: to love obscurity, attached as it was then to the thin fellow and world-beater-to-be in baggy trousers. Now what wouldn't you give to be, as the old song has it, "young and foolish again ..."

And there we were, Veinberg and Santos and me 17 years ago, hoping someday we'd be somebody, thinking how lucky we were to be in Paris with enough in our pockets to survive the fall. I thought of little beyond the lovely trees, shopping at the *fromagerie*, buying lamb and *Beaujolais nouveau*, returning our wine bottles to the little shop for 20 *centimes*.

17 years ago on these boulevards thinking about the great poets with Veinberg and Santos, knowing we weren't them, but that at least we had poetry pushing out the long phrases of our breath, breath we could see on autumn mornings as we walked down the promenade in the *Jardin des Plantes* between the barbered sycamores — happy in our old clothes after a night when we almost again did not drink too much after hours at the Dixie Melody, listening in that stone basement to someone as flawless and smoldering as Carmen McRae, and walking out of there to the early sun spiking the sleepless river....

Yesterday, I mailed them sentimental postcards of the autumn trees lining the Seine. I've been waiting 17 years to feel this way again. The pink neon still buzzes outside the Dixie Melody, the sidewalks wide and unending, and our lives, more or less, burning away imperceptibly like the little fragments of smoke from the chestnut vendor's coals. If we're lucky, we'll find ourselves on a street, stopping at a small table and happily ordering an over-priced coffee to watch the world go by a while, knowing there is nothing like it, nothing better, as long as we're here ...

Barbara Crooker
NOCTURNE IN BLUE

She asked me to bring her back a stone
from Paris, where even the dirt is historic,
but I wanted, instead, to find her the color
of *l'heure bleu*, the shimmer of twilight

with the street lamps coming on, the way they keep
the dark back for just a little while, the reflections
of headlamps and taillights, red and gold, on the Champs
d'Élysees wet with rain and a fog rising.

And there's the way the past becomes a stone,
how you carry it with you, lodged in your pocket.
The blue light deepens, evening's melancholy shawl,
the wide boulevard of the Seine, the way the stones

of the monuments become watery, ripple in the currents
and the wind. Everything seems eternal here,
to us from the West, who have no memory of dates
like 52 BC, 1066, the *fin de siècle*

as we barge on past the millennium,
history's crazy swirl, oil on pavement,
a promenade down *les Grands Boulevards*.
This is what I'd bring back: shadows of stones,

twilight longings, a handful of crushed lilacs
from the bar at the Closerie, some lavender de Provence,
Odilon Redon's chalky mauves, a jazz piano playing the blues,

Mood Indigo; just a condensation of blue,

distilled in a small glass bottle with a stopper,
as if it came from an expensive *parfumerie*,
musk of the centuries, the gathering dusk,
a hedge against night, the world that will end.

Barbara Crooker
IN PARIS

A rectangle of light spills in the high window
over the porcelain tub in our small *hôtel*,
and a blackbird, a *merle*, is singing his strange *chanson*,
r's swallowed in the back of his throat, those palate-
ringing u's: *dur, truffes, du fluide, tu penses.*
At the rue de Varenne, Rodin's Thinker is still stuck
in the rose garden, his bronze thoughts lost
in translation. Across the lawn, in a smaller version,
he broods above *les Portes d'Enfer*:
Abandon hope, all ye who enter.
Underneath, eternity's lovers twine
about each other, the embrace of the damned,
yearn and long but never touch, all that unattainable
flesh. The twisting lovers try to hold on even
as they are torn away or melt backwards
into the liquid bronze night, condemned to writhe
in tortured high relief. But we are here, in our
middle-aged imperfect bodies, walking hand in hand
under an *allée* of plane trees in the dazzled light,
and my desire for you, even after all these years,
is a *marc*, an *eau-de-vie*, hot and heady
in the blood. High above us, chimney swifts,
les martinets, take up their nightly chorus, shrieking
as they swoop and dive for insects in the long dusk.
Praise the small cage of the elevator
that carries us to our *chambre*. Praise my four-
chambered heart, still beating; praise your gall
bladder, unremoved. O Paris, city of *café noir*

and *vin rouge*, where even the subway signs
are works of art, city of rapturous light,
ghosts of Hemingway and Stein at the Closerie,
Simone and Jean-Paul at the Café de Flor,
you and I, our little story nearly over,
singing loudly as we can, in our tone deaf voices,
against the coming rain and the following dark.

Barbara Crooker
VOL DE NUIT/ NIGHT FLIGHT

Now, isn't that more elegant than *taking the Red-Eye?*
And don't you love it when the flight attendant
(Remember when she used to be a stewardess?
When everything matched her uniform, even her luggage,
and her makeup was heavy and impeccable?) hands
out pillows, blankets soft as babies' dreams, eye masks,
ear plugs — everything Mother would do but tuck you in
and read you a story. Or maybe she does — think of the fable
she recites at the beginning of the flight. Or did you think
it was true, that oxygen miraculously drops from above,
if the cabin pressure fails? That your seat cushion becomes a life
preserver if you fall into the black night of the North Atlantic?
That emergency lights will twinkle and glow, illuminate your path
to the exit chute, little constellations of hope? Never mind. Relax
into your backrest of many positions. Enjoy the multi-course
many-sectioned meal brought to you hot, without a kitchen in sight.
Hear the tinkle of the cart as she progresses down the aisle,
those cunning little bottles. Put on your headset, find the channel
with jazz or blues, unscrew the metal top, sip your red, and *voilà*,
you're in Paris already, hours ahead of time. So the *pâté* and *camembert*
come in tin foil, and the roll's hard as an iceberg. Thousands of miles
are rushing under your feet beneath these silver wings. Soon, you'll be racing
the dawn, as morning throws her rosy covers over the sky. *Briôches* and *café au lait,*
croissants and *café noir* will roll down the aisles. You'll begin your long descent
from the land of the clouds. Things may have shifted overhead. Everyone is speaking
in tongues, and none of them are yours. You must go to *le contrôle de passeports,*
and you will need to declare: business or pleasure. Someone is meeting
    you at the gate;

he's carrying a baguette and a single red rose, knows the minute your plane touches the tarmac. Now you have reclaimed your luggage, passed through customs, and entered the terminal, where your life begins again.

Barbara Crooker
AT THE CIMETIÈRE DE MONTMARTRE

We came down the hill from Montmartre,
disappointed that it was full of Americans
from the Place du Tertre to Sacré Coeur,
and ended up, at the lacy iron gates
of the cemetery, laid out like a small city,
long shady avenues, houses of marble and stone,
sunlight filtered through acacia trees.

We looked for the graves of the famous:
Berlioz, Truffaut, Émile Zola,
resting near the merely ordinary
in the dance of shadows and light. We sat
on a wrought iron bench, ate camembert,
pain de campagne, a kilo of cherries,
and for a sweet moment, I loved you so completely,
when I die, I want our ashes to mingle, bury us in earth,
plant a rose bush, let it grow thorny, tangled,
and covered in blossoms; I want there to be no
separation between my skin and yours.

Barbara Crooker
ARABESQUE

She sat at a small café in Paris, sunlight
filtering through the plane trees,
a dance of shadow and leaf.
Café filtré shimmered
in its small white cup.
At the Jardin de Luxembourg,
there were roses everywhere,
crinkled and ruched flirts
that sent their perfume
in envelopes of scent
on the soft air.
She was writing a letter,
but the words wouldn't come;
there was so much blue distance
between them. Up in the trees,
turtledoves blew their low notes,
songs flew easily from their beaks.
O, this dance of love, how it twists
and curlicues, the art deco sign
above the Métro, the many pathways
that wind to the heart.

Carly Sachs
A POEM ABOUT MEMORY OR DUST BUNNIES

This is before they are conceived. A memory not yet remembered. It was a certain song on a certain breezy evening with a man whose face is familiar as your own but you can't place the name, not until you take off your coat and then it comes to you. Like that. Paris 1973. Then there is your mother and she's calling you in. It's starting to rain. She's wearing that yellow apron, the one with the green ties. It's time for dinner. You forgot to sweep again. What's another week? To them it's an invitation. They come out of thin air and shadowed places. Like old lovers. You think they mate at night under your bed. They do it so quietly. You entertain the possibility that they also do it while you're at work. There are so many of them now, they shuffle around when you open the door or the window. Like your dead mother. They form packs and attempt to bite your heel. When you finally get to brooming, you have to pluck them from the straw, the soft grey matter. It reminds you of a cat and you are hungry.

Alison Jarvis
LISTEN

What I didn't expect was the cold
the first and last summer
we lived in Paris. The apartment in the eighth
you thought might be too grand was pure
opera — its tiny rooms; the fireplaces
needing fuel all June and July.
And how could I have expected you to move
through that summer on your own two feet?
Once, I read that longing, as a sickness of the heart,
is endless, incurable. In my story
you will always walk, you will always
play quartets, you will never be sick
and you will never really die.
                                    How did I manage
in my bad French, to rent a wheelchair?
When you had heartburn from all the pills you took
I asked the pharmacy to send us something
for a "fire in the heart."

Whatever the French celebrated that frozen summer,
it didn't matter, I was there layered
in unserious sweaters. On Bastille Day for the fireworks
at Trocadero, I wore three pairs of cotton socks and scarves
pulled around my neck, my breath in front of me.
I was wild to dance
at each Bastille Ball, in every firehouse,
in every quarter, stunned by wine,
no mind, no body.

Sometimes I used to think of us
as the two parts of that huge stone sculpture
out in front of St-Eustache: You, the poised
recumbent head, and me, the enormous hand,
a finger reaching for the sleeping cheek, longing
to stroke the body back ... *l'Ecoute*
it was called, the whorled ear
big enough for crawling into, cocked

to hear the whole world turning.

Nouvelles

Gauz
SALE AT CAMAÏEU

—— Translated by Tegan Raleigh

THE REGULARS. Buy clothes as if they were perishable goods. Come back every month, every week, every day, even several times a day. The regulars are easy to identify. They're always in a hurry. They know what they want. They never stay for long.

PSYCHEDELIC. Nothing else to see but the fiery spotlights of the false ceiling and the bright orange signs minted with the famous "%" symbol for sales. From a supine position in the stroller, this is baby's first psychedelic experience as the mom shops the sales racks.

HANDBAG. In a women's clothing store, there's no reason for a woman with a purse to spend any time in the silly little aisle of atrocious handbags... except to camouflage a theft. She crams her loot into her purse; and into one of the store's she stuffs the anti-theft devices she's pried off in the fitting rooms with the use of pliers. Unequal exchange of merchandise.

THE HANDBAG LAW. In a women's clothing store, all women are attached to their purses, especially those who are thieves.

CAMAÏEU AXIOM. In a clothing store, a client who doesn't have a purse is a client who won't steal anything.

CAMAÏEU RADIO: This is the music that is played in the store throughout the day. With Radio Camaïeu, out of every 10 songs an average of 7 are sung by women, 2 are duets between men and women, and just one is sung by a man. At about 3 minutes per song, or 20 songs per hour, the guard turns at 120 audio atrocities per 6-hour shift. The break was a great coup for the union.

RIGHT BUTTOCK. Even though it's possible to distinguish a few major categories, the shape of the buttocks is as unique as a fingerprint. Then the security guard starts thinking about what would go down at the police station if this had been the identification system chosen by the public authorities.

LEFT BUTTOCK. The Africans rarely get anything other than tops because of their callipygian anatomy. The pants as well as the shorts are based on the average measurements for white women, who are naturally flat, and manufactured by Chinese women workers, who are naturally very flat.

In China, it seems, there's no word for "buttock." Instead, people say "bottom of the back." You can't invent a word for a body part that doesn't exist.

CHINESE. With the enormous quantity of clothes produced in the country of Mao, you could say that it's a case of return to sender when there's a Chinese person in a clothing store.

DIALOGUE.
"Why are you hanging around me like that?" (The man.)
"Yeah, you're hovering. It's stressful!" (The woman.)
"I'm sorry, I'm not hanging around you. Not you in particular." (The security guard.)
"Wrong! Look in the stroller, there's nothing. Go hang around those French people over there instead. Not us."
"You're paranoid, sir."
"What?"
"You're par-a-noid."
"No I'm not. I'm Algerian."

ANTI-THEFT DEVICES, LABELS, AND FITTING ROOMS.

Women regularly emerge from the fitting rooms wearing outfits that they want to buy, their feet bare, to look for different sizes or colors. The clothes they're trying on are clearly embellished with various labels and broad, anti-theft circles made of gray plastic and shaped like flying saucers that are clamped right onto the fabric.

-*For sleeveless dresses*: a tag hangs under the armpits, an anti-theft device is attached to the right buttock, and the price is on the back.

-*For pants*: a tag on the right hip, another on the left thigh next to the discount (-50%, for example), which is on a long translucent ribbon stuck to the fabric. The price is on the left hip, and sometimes there's an additional "washing suggestions" tag suspended from a buckled strip in the back and poised over the crack.

-*For shirts and blouses*: The mark-down is a stripe on the left shoulder, a label is stuck on the left sleeve, the price emerges from the stomach.

For a woman who tries on *Carlita* jeans and a *Tolérant* top, this makes:

-24.95 euros, discounted at 50%, for the legs and the butt.

-14.95 euros, discounted at 30%, for the breasts and the torso.

Or a total reduced price of 17 euros and 45 centimes to package all secondary sexual characteristics.

HEAVY WOMEN. Often, heavy women start out trying on smaller clothes... before disappearing discreetly with the right size into the fitting rooms.

STOCKROOM. In the stockroom, there are bathrooms, personalized metallic lockers, a fridge, a microwave, and — most importantly — a board for internal communications, where the following has been written: "Difficult Week only in terms of sales revenue + Indicator + 9.91% = PRIME ☺ Stay mobilized!" (Punctuation and drawing duly copied)

SWEETEST LIL TOP. "Isn't this the sweetest lil top." This is one of the most commonly-used phrases to qualify the tops sold in the store. It is always spoken with the head lowered to tuck the "lil top" in question into the base of the neck with the chin while blinking the eyes and spreading it out over one's chest for display. The presence of an admiring interlocutor is optional.

GAULOISES TROPIQUETTES. These young, very flirtatious black girls spend hours in the store talking about clothes while they're buying them. A little bit like all these French people who talk about food at the table. Blood courses in our culture, not on the top of our skin.

CAPILLARY METAMORPHOSES. Fatima, the store manager, lost the pretty, black, North African ringlets that she had last week. Now her hair is as straight and blond as a lady Viking's.

The black saleslady, Christiane, has never revealed her beautiful, kinky hair. She wears a long synthetic weave of big, black curls that falls to the middle of her back.

PETROLEUM AND ALPHA-KERATIN. Over the course of two weeks standing watch over the store, not a single black woman with natural hair has come into the store. They always wear wigs, extensions, clip-ins, or weaves made of synthetic fibers produced by the petroleum industry. Petroleum, a source of energy across the globe, results from the decomposition, within the lower geological strata, of all the prehistoric organic matter that has accumulated over time. Black women wear fossil fuels on their heads.

The security guard sees a black woman with a long and voluminous mane of curls that reaches the tops of her thighs. At least one entire tribe of tyrannosaurs had to decompose for her to wear her hair like that.

THEORY OF CAPILLARY DESIRE. The contamination of capillary desire progresses in a northward direction: the *Beurette*, or girl of North African descent, wants the straight, blond hair of her Viking neighbor to the north, while the *Tropiquette* covets the *Beurette*'s curls.

BWWB: Bété Woman with White Babies. The security guard immediately recognizes the "Bété Women with White Babies." They come from the Ivory Coast, specifically the Gagnoa region. In France, they are almost all "assistant guardians."

ASSISTANT GUARDIAN. A well-chosen martial term to designate the nannies of these Occidental children that are half-royalty, half-prisoner.

TRADITIONAL BWWB. The security guard is struck by a crazy vision of a BWWB entering the store, her breasts bare and waist girded with the old-style skirt woven with the ribs of raffia fronds. But reality is quick to return. She's pushing a two-seater stroller with a pair of fair-haired angels sleeping inside. The BWWB is wearing a "sweetest lil top" in polyamide and old, worn-out jeans.

BWWB DIALOGUE.
"I don't buy wôro-wôro jeans[1*] that are just going to fall apart!" (BWWD 1 looking disdainfully at some stonewashed jeans.)
"You're right, Sis. What's the point of having holes in jeans before anybody even buys them? Tchrrrr!"[2**] (BWWD 2 approves).

VOCABULARY. The job of working as a security guard is so firmly anchored in the milieu of Cote d'Ivoiriens in France that it has generated a specific terminology, always colored with expressions from the Abidjan vernacular, Nouchi.

DEBOUT-PAYÉ (STAND-BY-THE-HOUR). Designates all jobs that require you to remain standing to earn your pittance.

ZAGOLI. Designates the security guard himself. Zagoli Golié is the name of a famous goalie for the Éléphants, the Ivory Coast's national soccer team. Working as a security guard is like working as a goalie: you stay standing to watch others play, and every so often you jump in to fetch.
SOUFÈ-WOURU: Literally "dog of the night" in Malinké, this term

---

1 Wôro-wôro: shared taxis in Abidjan, which are very rickety and always break down.
2 Tchrrrr!: a characteristic sound that Africans make by whistling, with lips and teeth pressed together, to express disgust.

designates the "dog masters," or the "security agent dog drivers," as per the administrative terminology. Even though they are much better paid, among the Africans there are far fewer "soufè-wouru"s than "zagoli"s.

In Sahelian as well as Subsaharan Africa, apart from a caste of hunters called the "Dozos," who dress up like scarecrows, canines are only considered with expressions such as "mangy dogs," "mongrels," "nasty mutt," etc. There is very little nuance in terms of the place they occupy in human society.

The notion of the dog being man's best friend is an all-too-recent *Occidentalism*. When you've grown up being contemptuous or afraid of the dogs, mostly mangy or rabid, that make their scrawny way through the African cities, resolving to have one as a life companion and work partner is a psychological and cultural obstacle that is very difficult to overcome. Plus, the initial financial investment of having a dog, feeding it, training it, and generally caring for is not negligible, especially when you don't have the right papers, or work. And if you've got to have one for work, you could say that the dog bites its own tail. The Ivorians have thus come to the conclusion that being a Zagoli is better.

RADIO CAMAÏEU 2

I like your body
So shake you booty
Let's get it on
And keep on pushing...

A great number of "neo soul" singers that are English, American, as well as French (the worst) dump mediocre lyrics into bland, diluted versions of the tortured but incredible Amy Winehouse.

As Aretha Franklin still walks this earth, how can anyone let these *sous-chanteuses* run around and say that what they're doing is soul music? There's no longer the time or the decency to let the greats turn in their graves. From now on, we insult them while they're still alive.

FLOWER POWER. Laura and Rosa, two joyful Caribbean sales

clerks with the names of flowers. From time to time, they improvise graceful dance moves to the airs of Radio Camaïeu. When they let loose, it never fails to put a smile on the lips of every employee in the store and magically attenuates the lack of talent of those women yammering from the speaker system, if only for just a few measures.

FIRST THEORY OF CARIBBEAN GENETICS. Skin color, eye color, type of hair, shape of the nose, the mouth, the rear... Caribbean people always have at least one physical feature that serves as a reminder that the white master, the Béké, didn't wield just his whip with his women slaves. Perhaps it would be more appropriate to say "his females," so as to be in keeping with the language of the era.

SECOND THEORY OF CARIBBEAN GENETICS. During the time of slavery, it was extremely rare — impossible, in fact — for a black male slave to reproduce with the white mistress. It was thus the white masters that mixed the races in the Caribbean. Since it's the man who gives the male child his sex with his Y chromosome, it can be affirmed that all men of mixed race from the Caribbean are certain to have a Y chromosome of Caucasian origin.

Simply put, according to the theory, man is white and woman is black in the Caribbean.

BABIES. They're fascinated by everything and always end up making the guard smile.

The security guard loves babies. Maybe because babies don't steal.

The babies love the security guard. Maybe because he doesn't drag babies to sales.

ENGLISH VERSION. Because of the high volume of foreign tourists, the shopping bags for numerous stores translate the French word "soldes" into English, as with the bags from the neighboring Lacoste store, which say: SALES. A fellow security guard from the adjacent store talks of French families that refuse to take these bags. It seems they don't want to leave

---

Translator's Note: SALES reads as "DIRTY" in French

themselves open to any linguistic confusion that could lead to negative ideas about their personal hygiene.

LES MOUSTACHUES. A mother and her daughter who look a lot alike both have a fine, quite visible moustache. The girl is still a teen who sulks and gives a strong impression of being profoundly discontented with life. The mother is in her fifties and though she's more somber, seems happier. She's had to put up with having hair where most women don't for decades, probably since she was as old as her daughter is now, and she's had ample time to figure out how to accept it or at least to make do. The girl still has a few more years to learn the ropes.

The mustachioed mother and daughter came a second time. They're easy to recognize. The security guard throws a "bonjour" topped with a big smile their way with dim hopes of cheering them up. The mother doesn't respond and doesn't even take the time to turn around. The girl gives the security guard the stinkeye.

THEORY OF THE MOUSTACHE. Hitler, Stalin, Pinochet, Bongo, Saddam Hussein... As much as the moustache is, for the dictator, an external sign of personal fulfillment, it's a source of malaise for women, especially adolescents.

NEW LOOK TODAY, HEIRESS TOMORROW. After wandering around the store for more than an hour and ultimately buying nothing, a woman speaks to a very old woman who's bent over her cane. "Maman, let's go across to New Look for the latest markdown."

The old woman is visibly exhausted in the canicular heat of summer. Her mouth is open but she doesn't skip a beat and plods after her daughter.

LAPLACE TRANSFORMS. How can anyone end up thinking about "Laplace transforms" while watching an old lady with pale violet hair ransacking the aisle of ugly *Gaby* cardigans, 70% off the tag price of 24.95€, that are the same beige as goose poop?

TATTOOS. The fine, precise strokes of the tattoo on her neck represent a lotus that has the same design as the logo for the "Lotus" brand of toilet paper. With her very pale skin, it's a little as if she had a roll of TP between her head and shoulders.

RETROREVOLUTION. In the popular imagination of the West, piercings, scarifications, and tattoos have long represented the quintessence of the remotest savagery.

Today, what does it mean to have all this white skin impaled from all directions? All these tribal tattoos? Is it a style, a malaise? The style of malaise? The malaise of style? The unconscious desire to return to the reassuring state of the "innocent savage"?

REVOLUTION. It is now known that there were only 7 haggard prisoners being kept in the Bastille on July 14, 1789. In other words, there was hardly anyone to set free. But History is more liable to retain symbols than facts. If it were to take place again today, the storming of the Bastille would liberate thousands of people who are prisoners of consumerism.

LAPLACE TRANSFORMS 2. It's a complex mathematical operation, invented by the eponymous scientist, that makes it possible to describe the temporal variations of certain functions. These days, this operation is used to establish prices. Laplace transforms, for example, are used to find the optimal markdowns and prices to apply when there is a sale going on. Such a complicated matter for such frivolous things.

IPHONE. A little girl is trying on glasses and she looks at herself using Facetime on her iPhone. Next to her, there's a big mirror that reaches all the way from the ceiling to the floor.

Girls try outfits on in the fitting rooms and take pictures of themselves from all angles with their iPhones. Then they discuss their choices while gathered around the screen. The pixel has taken power over the retina.

CHRISTLIKE. One arm extended towards the *Crayfish linen* skirts, the other reaching for the *Laure summer* dresses, a woman is on her knees before the *Victoire* miniskirts. Amen.

BLASPHEMY. On the rack of stirrup pants, there are a dozen that aren't "Made in China." They're "Made in Turkey." That's practically Europe!

THE ANGEL. Place de la Bastille: above its obelisk, the golden Angel is always nude. Since angels are asexual, they can get their clothes either way at Camaïeau or Celio. How to tell them that sale season is on now?

DIALOGUE.
"How much is a 20% reduction, please?" (The woman brandishes a label that's marked 29,99 €.)
"Around 6 euros, Madame." (The security guard.)
"Ah, you know, you've got to take pride in what you wear, get a taste for life again. I just lost my husband."
"…!"
"Merci monsieur. You're too kind. I'm going to the register now."

THE TEEN IN THE CHAIR. A disabled teenager is in a motorized wheelchair. Her sister's in front and she's followed by her mother and father. At the back of her chair is a bar to be used if she needs a push. In the store, the bar serves as a place to hang the clothes that she and her sister choose frenziedly. After an hour, the wheelchair looks like a mobile Camaïeu clothing rack.

LOVERS. The lovers are kissing greedily in the corner of the *Jakartas*, long dresses in bright colors that, here, are reminiscent of the curtains in a brothel. On Radio Camaïeu, Brick and Lace sing "Love is Wicked."

THE MODEL. *Striped Baléar* on top, *Martinique* pants below, *Artémis* on the feet, a woman decked out entirely in Camaïeu enters the store.

HADÈS. *Hadès*, a 100% pigskin jacket. Is such a jacket forbidden for Muslims and Jews?

"*Hadès*, the Haram jacket." (The Grand Mufti.)

"*Hadès*, the unkosher jacket." (The Chief Rabbi.)

"'70% off' the 100% pigskin jacket, at 99,95 euros: *Hadès* jacket, the discount of temptation. (The Super Chain.)

DEFINITIONS.

98% cotton + 2% elastane = Skinny jeans.

95% cotton + 5% elastane = Stirrup pants.

3% elastane is the formula for being cool or to be unfashionable.

ARTICLE NAMES.

Mystic: top.

Tolérant: top.

Égypte Deux: dress.

Rigolo: top.

Jane: jean.

Striped Tabata: dress. Tabata was the pseudonym of a famous porn actress from the 90s.

Martinique: White linen pants. At the time of slavery in Martinique, the Békés wore these kinds of pants on the sugarcane plantations.

Toronto, Denver, San Francisco, Dakar: dresses. In the aisles of Camaïeu, Dakar is next to San Francisco.

JEANS. A jean called *Jane*.

THE "NAMERS." With all of this literature on the clothing, in the Camaïeu flow charts there are positions for "namers": specialists who christen dresses and pants of all kinds.

THE "NAMERS" 2. When the security guard imagines what a meeting of the three "namers" is like: they're seated around a table, coupes of champagne in their hands, silver buckets full of caviar. The clothes scroll past them on hangers that are attached to a motor-driven metallic cord. A floral dress goes by. Between two swigs of "La Veuve Cliquot," a "namer" bellows solemnly, "You shall be called Hibiscus. Next!" The two others nod their heads in agreement, faces serious and mouths full of sturgeon eggs. Another dress slides into view.

VIRTUOSOS OF VISCOSE. Hummingbird, Crayfish, Tapir, at 92%, 95%, and 98% viscose, respectively... the higher the concentration of viscose, the more bizarre the animal the "namers" choose to christen their clothes.

RADIO CAMAÏEU 3

I like the way you shake your ass around me
I like the way you swing your lips around me...

Radio Camaïeu sings into the ears of an old woman. She moves her hips softly and wags her head while digging through the -70% dresses, the biggest markdown to date.

"%". Like a dick in between its gonads, the "%" sign, imprinted on numerous placards hanging from the false ceiling, hover above the heads of all these women excited by the sales.

POLYMER. Polyester, polyamide, polyvinyl... are the large synthetic molecules that are the basis of the fibers used in the textile industry. The chemists call them "polymers."
With maternity remote and sexual life on the decline, women over 50 are attracted by clothes made of polyester, polyamide, and polyvinyl fibers. The security guard calls them "poly-mères."

HIDE-AND-SEEK. To be suspicious of a security guard who is bored or who seems to be.
To pass the time, sometimes the security guard plays hide-and-seek with a thief.
The security guard hides from the thief so as to catch her in the act.

The thief hides from the security guard so as to not be caught in the act.

The amount of time that a thief spends to pilfer some 20,95 € shoes that are discounted at -30%! After two hours of hide-and-seek, if the thief's larceny is successful, she still needs the time to sell them, in the best-case scenario at around half of their value. With the risks, the skills, and an average of 3 hours per article from the theft to the resale, you could say that being a "Camaïeu thief" is not particularly lucrative.

HIDE-AND-SEEK 2. Hide-and-seek in the racks for the long dresses: the favorite game of restless children.

THE TEEN IN THE CHAIR 2. The father helps the teen get out of her chair and walk to the fitting rooms. These hands that slide over these bodies, these arms that enlace and interlace, embrace, support… There's a lot of tenderness between this father and this girl. They're connected both by father-daughter love and the girl's physical dependence. In reality, the two of them support one another. Dependence isn't always where you expect it. Do beings that have to touch each other so often develop above-average tenderness and gentleness? Would we be gentler to one another if we had greater physical contact?

THE BLIND WOMAN. Accompanied by her husband, her daughter, and her dog, a blind woman shops the sales. The man speaks to her loudly the whole time in his accent from the south, using well-formed, precise sentences. She strokes the fabrics unhurriedly to make her choice. From time to time, he touches her discreetly to point her in the right direction. Again, interdependence. Again, a lot of gentleness. The woman's limitation is a factor in improving the language of her clan.

MECHANICS OF THE TEEN'S CHAIR.
- 2 front drive wheels
- Electric motor
- Large lithium battery
- 2 rear guide wheels
- Seat topped with a green fluorescent shell to support the back

- Ingenious storage system on the sides and beneath the chair
- Directional joystick and liquid crystal mini control screen on the right armrest
- 4 buttons below the joystick, one with the image of a trumpet.

Is the teenager's chair a precursor to the car of the future? It's a far cry from the 4-wheeled boards that polio sufferers and people without legs used to use.

BIOMECHANICS OF THE SECURITY GUARD. By what biomechanical paradox does the security guard have coccyx pain even though he's standing all day long?

BIOLOGY OF THE SECURITY GUARD. Urgent tenesmus... One hour before the break, this violent desire to take a piss.

MULTILINGUAL. On a big sign at the back of the store are the words: SALDI, ZL'AVY, SOLDEN, ARLESZALLITAS, WYPRZEDAZ, SLEVY, OCTAKИ, REDUCERI, PROMOTIONALE, REBAJAS... Europe is also taking shape through consumerism.

ÉLISABETH. This is an anorexic-looking saleswoman who has to distribute her 80 pounds over 5 and a half feet. She's very energetic and never misses the opportunity to pointedly wink or throw her prettiest smile to the guard, who weighs around 220 pounds. Natural attraction of polar opposites.

ÉLISABETH 2. Before going home, the security guard distributes Carambar® caramels to all the saleswomen in the store. Élisabeth gets two.

WHEN THE MUSIC STOPS. 7:30 PM, when the music stops...
The metallic sound of the hangers running along the rails of the clothes racks: the girls are putting things away. The last clients are taking things out. Polite but firm, the guard has to lead them towards the register while making sure that no new clients come in. It's the grand splits at the end of the show. Inside, there are always those who swear

on whatever's dearest to them that they'll just be there two minutes more. At the entrance, there are always those who swear on whatever's dearest to them that they'll just take two minutes. They always have a hard time getting turned down by the people they don't see during the day. Everything's on sale, including self-respect.

Jean-Paul Clébert
THE BAWDYHOUSE FOR BEGGARS

—— Translated by Edward Gauvin

Before the war there was, I think, in the St.-Paul neighborhood on rue de Fourcy, a most astonishing public space, a whorehouse for hobos. This bedlam, now vanished from the earth if not its clients' memories, and whose sorely missed atmosphere can be readily imagined, consisted of two rooms — the Senate, where the rate was ten francs across the board, and the House of Representatives, where it hovered, according to mood and quality, around fifteen. It is pleasant to listen to an old woman who thought to live out her days as a pensioner there try and recover her memories of the extraordinary comico-heroic theatre that went on: an old panhandler with formidable whiskers making a racket, making threats, shaking his fist at some low-rent floozy, howling in a voice more-than-soused at her face: ten francs? You tart! You're not even worth twenty centimes…

Now: how, where, when, with whom do they make love, the tramps and vagabonds of this big city, the everyday collapsees of metro seats, waiting rooms, hospitable bistros, squares, avenues, alive and well and sleeping head to toe at the feet of stairwells, in the corners of porte-cocheres, on church steps, on park lawns, beneath the bridges of the Seine and on the quaysides of canals, wherever there's a shady, solitary spot; how do these folks who almost always manage to rustle up a crust of bread, a can of soup, a liter of red — how do they get some? Not the old ones, who don't care anymore, settling now and then, whenever a chance is in reach, for stretching out beside some aging vagrant whose thighs are still white beneath her reeking black rags, the skin of her belly still soft despite the gray hairs: someone who, deep in the smell of booze, filth, whiffs of cigarette butts and rotten breath, soon gets her hips back in the swing of things, recalls the slow caresses, and amidst a barrage of profanities, the sighs and whispers that punctuate an amorous embrace. Not the old folks, but the young ones. That is, if they're not built like spiffy sailor boys marauding along fairground shores, if they're not more or less well-dressed and presentable despite no-meal-in-three-days, and manage to "do" maids right outside the movies or ugly girls outside their offices — how do they get some? A mystery difficult to fathom, for none are more discreet than the destitute, and many get their satisfaction with each other, many make do just dreaming about it, one eye wide, and gazing at posters, pinups, stars, bra models, panty dummies, pairs of legs flying flesh-colored hose — advertising having, as it does, standards that surpass their fantasies. How many times have I hung around town, tapped out down to the last crumb, not stopping in front of charcuterie windows anymore but lingerie boutiques instead — yeah, me too, staring vacantly but piercingly at the splendid photos of splendid girls, with their beguiling bosoms sculpted in soft cloth, then hopelessly feasting my eyes on every woman that walks by, sitting on a bench and keeping a naïve tally — the kind you laugh about later — of all the ones who might have, well...

On the Quai de la Tourelle, I watch a pervert who's just approached a ragpicker, a woman. He's got the mug for it: middle-aged, turned-up collar, hands in pockets. He must've offered her money to get his rocks off on her, and now she's giving him an earful. Neither young nor old, she's a drifter, dirty, her legs sheathed in black varicose veins and red splotches. Bastard, she yells, I'm no whore, I don't want your money! Bugger off, you filthy animal! Hands off! But the guy insists, keeps following her. She threatens him with a fist, a bottle. Don't give a fuck about your stupid dough, you piece of trash, my ass is my own, it's cleaner than yours. I don't fuck nutjobs, and I'm no floozy, I tell you, I'm not for sale, so beat it, you worthless trash!

I go over and the guy steps back into the shadows between the trees. He's pulled out his tool, which he points at the vagrant, who spits at him, disgusted. Beat it, she screams, or I'll break you in two. The guy straightens himself up and drifts off. She comes toward me. It's Mimi, from the Magasins Généraux. Of course, she launches into an endless commentary on this sordid story. Guys like that, they're coming out of the woodwork, I'm telling you, off their rockers and twisted too, they should lock'em all up, I can't even sleep easy with them lurking around here anymore, the sons of bitches. Would've killed'im if I'd had my man with me. And she adds, with a knowing air: Probably some American.

Jessie Vail Aufiery
DIABOLO MENTHE

Ludo strained through trikonasana and downward facing dog, sweat dripping onto his purple mat. As usual, he had to marshal the sum of his physical and mental forces to keep up with Jean-Luc's barked commands; a row ahead, the girl in yellow shorts shifted fluidly from one posture to the next. Jean-Luc was a barefoot Napoleon, eyes flashing as they scanned the room. "Lift the kneecaps!" he shouted. "Kneecaps in!"

Ludo contracted the fronts of his thighs and wondered what the girl in yellow shorts thought of the teacher. Compact and sleek as soap, the little man oozed sexuality even as he recalibrated sweating students with nudges of his fingers and toes. He wondered what his wife would make of Jean-Luc. He and Jen made love only a couple of times a week, and for that she had to be cajoled, but every day he felt his body's demand for release. Sometimes he suspected her of pleasuring herself on the sly while he dealt with traffic and ball-busting clients, keeping the leaky ship that was their family afloat.

After class he pulled on his street clothes. People changed quickly and didn't linger in the center's ad hoc changing room. The girl in yellow shorts, her small breasts barely concealed under a sports bra, was trying to untangle a barrette from her dark curls.

"*Merde*," she said, looking up at him. "Can't get this out."

His hands trembled as they freed the trapped strands from the thick silver hinge. A scent of apricots clung to his fingers.

"You could keep things in there," he said, gesturing at her thick spiraling hair. "Wallet, keys…"

"My god," the girl said, eyes wide. "I blow it dry, brush it. It does what it wants."

"At least this way if you ever got kidnapped," he said, "you could just pull out a screw driver out and jimmy the trunk."

"Or a pillow," the girl said. "For a little nap."

"A cigarette to smoke before your execution."

The girl smiled, a blush creeping up her neck.

"You have beautiful eyes," she said.

"They come from a rare eyes dealer," he said, feeling a jolt at his groin. "At the flea market behind the carpets…"

She put a hand in front of her mouth and laughed. He slung his backpack over one shoulder and said:

"I should get your number."

Her eyes, surprised, flickered over his left hand. He thought she would pretend she hadn't seen the gold band but she smirked and asked: "What about your wife?"

"Hmm, better not," he said. "My wife doesn't hand her number out to strangers."

Outside he descended into the metro, jumped on a train, and waited for his connection at Champs Elysées. The train thundered up, brakes whining. A dark-skinned, black teenager wearing headphones stood gently rocking. *Young enough to be my son*, Ludo thought idly. *If I'd started early.* The train rumbled on. Ludo felt a tugging of eyes, an oppressive sensation of being observed. He glanced to the side and was startled by his reflection in the glass. Not bad for forty. He hadn't flirted in ages, and the exhilarated feeling was only slightly marred by the fact that he was now stuck on public transportation. As the train eased into Varenne station, Rodin's *The Thinker*, a ragged hole in its hollow right thigh, glided into view like a snapshot. The hydraulic brake-release hissed, and the train rolled forward again. At the next station a group of high school students crowded into the wagon. A tall boy with a Catholic medal, one of the newcomers, said loudly in French: "Whoever's doing that, you'd better stop pinching my ass."

A few beats of silence and everyone laughed. The boy's shirt was open to the third button, and he wore a silk scarf loosely knotted over his bare chest. Amazing how people continued to accessorize, even in this heat. Ludo noticed a crucifix dangling alongside the medal, and he briefly loathed the handsome, dark-haired kid though he couldn't think why.

He arrived home to find his wife's easel set up in the living room next to the French windows, the floor covered in newspaper and tubes of paint. The easel had that just out-of-the-box look, all unblemished pine. Boris must be at one of his activities. Monday was judo, or perhaps drama. The living room reeked of stale coffee and turpentine rags, and his wife's canvas was heavy with slabs of saturated color. Looking at the thick globs, he thought of the money she spent chasing fantasies. She'd started introducing herself to new acquaintances as an artist: the first step in making something happen, she said, was in believing it *could* happen. He wanted to hold her from behind, work her pants down with one hand while unclasping her bra with the other and playing with her breasts. Where was she?

The drapes were yanked to the side, and the windows open. Across the street, curtains ballooned against the neighbor's wrought-iron balcony. The man often appeared in a kimono, his gray-streaked hair disheveled, sniffing the air with his large Roman nose. Ludo had noticed him reading a paperback on the town square. Waiting, he supposed, for salvation to appear out of the ether: a girlfriend, a job, a spaceship to the moon. Now through the gauzy curtains he discerned the gray-streaked mane, and also a familiar figure, hands gesticulating expansively. *Putain de merde*. This absurd reaching out to strangers was unbearable! Last time she had introduced herself to a slovenly Scotsman just because the guy and his girlfriend were speaking English in the beer aisle. Why did she do it? It wasn't hard to see what happened: his wife painting with the French windows wide, the neighbor just across at *his* window, each trying to catch a breeze in this stifling heat, it was natural to exchange a wave of neighborly greeting, and then, very casual, Bonjour! I couldn't help noticing that you're painting! Did you catch that marvelous Freud retrospective at the Pompidou? I have the catalogue. Come have a look, if you'd like...

Squinting, he saw wine glasses and a bottle, heads bobbing in animated conversation. His wife was always complaining about how hard it was to adapt, the emptiness of her days when he was at work and their son at school. She had dropped her painting class despite the non-refundable fee because she said the other students were all doing "boutique art" and she wanted to do something real, maybe even installations. It was boredom, he knew that, a lack of purpose. She was too proud to get in with the other mothers as they gathered at the café each morning, never inviting her, and there was no one else to talk to. If they had stayed in New York, she said, she would have a job and friends. Her parents would be within driving distance. She'd belong to the co-op.

He thought with pleasure of the girl in the yellow shorts, young and smiling. Through the window he saw the neighbor staring intently at his animated wife, his head bobbing in agreement. The fraud! As if he gave a damn about what combination of words came out of her mouth. Ludo did a quick run-through of his options. He could call to her through the window, ring up her cell phone, pound on the fraud's door... All of which would make him look like a jealous fool. He couldn't let her find him here seething: couldn't confront her until he'd settled on revenge.

He slammed out of the apartment and stormed down the street to the Café des Sports. In three gulps he downed a Kronenbourg 1664 and signaled for another. Someone had left a copy of *Paris Match*, and he flipped through pictures of Carla Bruni and *monsieur le president* as he drank. Young beautiful woman, nasty stunted rat. Hope enough to go around. As dusk settled, he realized he was tipsy. He also noticed he had wrenched his shoulder, the one that always gave him trouble. Past the cool window, the town's city hall was wedged like some blasted planet against the cobalt sky. Several yards in front of this, a grim fountain misted the faces of passerby.

Ah, familiar faces! Mothers with children who prattled relentlessly about the latest trombone lesson or judo slam across the dojo floor. Bureaucrats trailing the ghost of their thirty-five hours. A blue-suited city worker manning the wheel of a small truck while his partner, high above on a mechanical ladder, screwed light bulbs into street lamps. A drunk struggling with the door to the public toilet. Children kicking balls and jumping rope. All these frenetic silhouettes — actors in a shadow play — reminded Ludo of his wife laughing with strange men, of his bank account filling and emptying in a cyclical tide. Outside, friends and neighbors plodded forward as if this shadow life was real, buying houses, businesses, investing their lives...

He took out his cell phone and dialed. Upon hearing his voice she said a happy Oh, hello! and he felt a wonderful galloping like horses over roses. Her name was Natasha, and she agreed to meet tomorrow...

He arrived early and ordered an espresso. The café, a few steps from Natasha's apartment, she'd explained, was of her choosing. Two men, kids really, sat at a nearby table. Both had their phones out. Next to Ludo, a twenty-year-old in a leather porkpie hat kissed his tattooed girlfriend. The soul of pretension! Ludo writhed in inner discomfort. Everywhere he looked, he saw stupidity, ugliness.

Conscious of his suit and tie he drank an espresso and manipulated his Blackberry. Last night he'd lain awake horny and sweating in the terrible heat while his wife refused to come to bed. As if his display of anger when she returned flushed with wine and accomplishment made *him* the villian.

"But I invited him to dinner Saturday," she protested.

"Well, *un*invite him."

He remembered coming to this very café with his son, Boris, after sailing a rented toy boat around the fountain at the *Jardin de Luxembourg.* Looking like a small man in a black pea coat and scarf, Boris had marched in and announced to the girl behind the bar: "I'm having a diabolo menthe!"

The girl had laughed and brought over a glass one-third filled with green syrup, and a bottle of Sprite.

"*Enfin,*" she said as she set it in front of Boris, who was sitting as straight-backed as a miniature Mao Tse-Tung. "A man who knows what he wants."

Ludo had loved this generalissimo moment, and guarded the memory of it like a jewel. His son: the bright child of a spoiled, overeducated, endlessly encouraging American mother; this son, unbowed by the trailing burden of *la France*, would know how to command.

The café door opened and his heart flew.

No. This was a woman in her forties, trying too hard in stilettos and a tulle skirt. Her friends leaned toward her admiringly, exclaiming: "Wo-ow." The place was crawling with artsy types. His wife could bring the neighbor and look deep into his fraudulent, Neanderthal eyes.

A head of dark curls was moving toward him. Natasha. Wearing a tight sweater and Converse high tops. Away from the yoga studio, she looked different. She dropped a book onto his table and grinned. *Introductory Chemistry*, a college textbook. A queasy feeling shivered through him: she was younger than he thought. Then he noticed her thick brows slanting in a way that made him think of a Renoir—one of those soft-faced Michelin nudes—and he visualized a dark muff of hair between her legs.

"Coucou!" she said, tapping the table with the big ring she wore on her forefinger.

"Sorry," he smiled, standing to kiss her cheeks. "Seeing you makes me think I might do something I'll regret."

"Regret?" she laughed, raising her hand for the waiter. "Coming from you, that sounds funny. Come on, let's order drinks…"

Walking to the metro he stopped to gaze at a lumpy bronze statue of a soldier, *Capitaine Dreyfus*. Dreyfus stood with a broken-off sword in one hand, and a pigeon fluffed on his brimmed cap. At the statue's base a plaque in French said: If you wish me to live, have them give me back my honor.

Ludo picked up a bottle cap and chucked it at the pigeon, his shoulder flaring in pain. The pigeon flapped to a branch, dust motes spinning in the silvery light.

A jogger thudded past.

American, he estimated, as her firm buttocks and pink thighs wobbled past, a baseball cap tucked low over her eyes. Who else runs down the middle of the street?

Massaging the shoulder, he descended into the metro. In California everyone wore baseball caps and jogged. His own memories of a childhood trip to the Golden State were foggy, though he retained the image of a waitress setting down a tall stack of fluffy pancakes topped with maple syrup and whipped cream. Ludo felt if he returned to California — now, today — the state's sunshine would wrap itself around him like a long-awaited homecoming embrace.

His train arrived and he hurried on. As it lurched forward he lost his balance and stumbled over a girl's white sneaker. The girl: a sallow, lank-haired Parisian, glared like he was an assassin. He smiled, thinking of Natasha, who, in hindsight, seemed almost more American than his wife. In California he and Natasha could wear baseball caps and go jogging. They could politely ignore the movie stars who were also jogging, and when they had jogged the requisite five miles, they could stop at IHOP and order a tall-stack with bacon, after which they could hit the beach and watch the crashing golden waves…

The train slid into *Varenne*. Ludo noted that a metal patch had been soldered over the hole in The Thinker's thigh, leaving a thin uncovered strip: an entrance for a family of cockroaches. Even people repairing master artworks in this country were incompetent! As he swayed in the overcrowded wagon, he felt his mood plunge.

At home he swung the door open, his keys jangling in the lock. His wife was perched in front of her easel, and her silent profile made him want to slam the door until it fell off its hinges. But this was his home and not a monkey house, even if his wife insisted on acting like an ignorant ape. He pulled the door to until it gave a soft click. He dropped his briefcase, shed his clothes and showered, the hot water drumming his shoulder, the pain that was now radiating up his neck. After the shower he slicked back his hair, poured a tumbler of Bailey's on ice, and walked towel-waisted into the living room. Jen was still working away, and it occurred to him, dim hope igniting in his chest, that she might be inspired to strip away his towel. He dropped onto the couch and pointed the remote at the television, his body radiating a moist heat.

"Do you mind?"

"No," he said, flicking past CNN and the 24-hour airport channel.

She sighed and squeezed out some white paint. Through his peripheral vision he noted that the curtain was closed, and that she looked pinched and pale. This was deeply satisfying: perhaps, for once, she felt chastened. He found a UFC match, turned up the volume, and took a long swallow of his drink. Two guys beating each other bloody. His wife smeared a gob of paint onto her canvas. The sweet icy liquid flowed down his throat, and he tossed a cushion onto the coffee table and propped up his feet. Then he was up again to retrieve the nail-clippers and then back to the couch and deeply concentrated on clipping the thick nails and sweeping them into a mound next to his drink. It felt good to be clean. He closed his eyes and imagined this was the start of being relaxed.

Then he opened them and realized his wife was staring, her mouth open.

"You're a pig, you know that?"

He held her gaze for a long moment, chuckling and watching her face redden as it became apparent he wouldn't dignify her attack with a response. Finally he broke eye contact, gathered the clippings into his palm, and dumped them into the ficus. Amidst the hoots and applause of the UFC crowd, the boom of the American announcer's voice, he dressed and walked outside into the heat.

The sky drooped. Three workers with grit clinging to their bare arms were installing an awning above a pizzeria, tools scattered across the sidewalk. Massaging his shoulder, he walked to the metro, imagining the relief of a cold beer flowing down his parched throat.

On the train an old man suddenly grabbed at the air and tumbled at Ludo's feet. Ludo stared down in bewilderment while a woman leapt forward and crouched at the man's side. The old man's wife gaped, her hands clutching shopping bags. The old man convulsed briefly and opened his eyes, very blue, confused.

"It's the heat," someone said, and the man was ushered out at the next station, flanked by his wife and the Good Samaritan. As the metro pulled away, the two old people were staring straight ahead, white-faced, backs erect. Ludo looked at his shoes, the ridged floor where the man had fallen. I should have done something, he thought. Shown initiative, taken control... *How long until he was just a white head staring into the abyss?* He wanted a drink, to lie down, to feel the coolness of fingers in his hair...

Outside, the humid air assaulted him. He found the blue door and the name: N. Bontemps. She rang him up on the third buzz, and a wave of apricot incense rushed his nose as she opened the door.

"I was listening to music," she said. "How long were you ringing?"

"I needed to see you."

"Oh." Her cheeks turned pink.

His eyes began to itch as she led him inside. A giant loft bed with a ladder took up most of the floor space; they sat into the couch that was wedged underneath it.

"Do you have anything to drink?" he said, tugging at his collar.

She jumped up. "Tap water okay?"

"Anything wet," he said, picturing the gently sweating bottles his wife kept stocked in the fridge.

The water tasted tinny. Her brows jumped as he drained the glass, his throat clicking. "Excuse me," he said.

She laughed behind her fingers. He wiped his mouth and set down the glass. Outside a bird chirped, and a motorbike could be heard bombing around a corner, its tires squealing. A tremor flickered across one of her eyelids, her gaze steady on his face. Quiet descended. He leaned in and kissed her. She curled into him, climbing his calves with her toes. He was suddenly charged up, light and strong. He pulled her close, tilting his head to change the angle of the kiss, and his neck made a soft *click* and blasted him with pain. *Putain*.

"Come," she said, slithering up the ladder to the loft.

He followed, his shoulder and neck electrified: stage-one of a searing discomfort he knew would last for days. A large white cat luxuriated across the rumpled sheets. Natasha removed her shirt, her eyes locked on his. He moved toward her on his knees, his head bumping the ceiling, and reached for her small firm breasts.

"Lie down," she commanded.

He did, and she removed his pants, caressing him through his shorts. He tried to concentrate on her fingers' light touch, her lips moving down his belly. His eyes and throat itched, and there was a planet of pain somewhere behind his right ear.

He stared at the greasy marks on the ceiling as she took him into her mouth and felt himself receding inside the pain; in panic, he directed his gaze downward and saw a pale mushroom poking out of his black pubic mound. Neck leaping in agony, he pushed himself into a sitting position.

"My neck," he said. "It does this thing—"

"*Relax*," she said. "Give it a minute."

His hand twitched with the sudden impulse to strike her. Natasha gazed at Ludo, her legs folded beneath her. The cat stood and rattled its fluffy tail. Suddenly he knew: it wasn't going to happen; he didn't *want* it to happen. Exhaustion settled over him like an itchy blanket. How tedious to have to justify oneself, to explain. He stared at Natasha, hoping to convey it all with his eyes. She gazed back at him with a limpid softness, and then stifled a sudden yawn. *She was bored*, he realized. *Bored but too busy playing the seductress to know it.* His hand twitched again. Youth made people stupid. He threw a leg over the edge of the loft, and started down the ladder.

A nervous giggle came from above: "Where are you going?"

He sweated all the way through trikonasana, but this time energy surged up his body past his nearly healed shoulder, all the way through his fingertips. Jean-Luc walked the room, tapping students' feet to nudge them into alignment. Ludo examined the teacher's hairless shins as the teacher lingered, eyeing him for fault.

Finally Jean-Luc said: "This shows an understanding of the posture."

Ludo's blood surged with vindication.

In the changing room, half-moons of sweat showed on Natasha's yellow shorts. She glanced over as he walked in, then averted her eyes and made a show of rummaging in her bag. Relieved, he pretended not to notice her.

At home he found his wife working on a watercolor. The carnival-like beeping of a video game drifted in from their son's bedroom. His wife's watercolor—pastel clouds over a golden sea—reminded Ludo of childhood summers in Brittany. On impulse, he crouched and placed his head on Jen's lap. He felt a slight shift in her posture and the weight of her hand, tentative, on the top of his head.

Thaddeus Rutkowski
PARDON MY FRENCH

When I arrived in Paris by train, I tried to place a call to a friend, someone I knew from my home city. Surprisingly, there was a phone service with a human attendant in the train station. I gave the phone woman the number I wanted to reach, and she dialed it.

Suddenly, she started yelling "*Occupé!*" at me. I thought she was telling me to get lost, so I started to walk away. She yelled more loudly and pointed at the phone. Slowly, I came to understand that "*Occupé*" meant "The line is busy." Presently, she put the call through. I took the phone from her and waited for an answer.

•

My friend came in a car to pick me up. He had the car for his job: He ran errands for a commercial production company, and he lived in the commercial director's apartment. As he drove, I watched green areas and monumental buildings swing through my field of vision.

Soon, we arrived at the commercial director's home: a converted storefront near the Bastille site. The apartment was large, with a spiral staircase connecting floors. I lugged my backpack up the metal steps and laid it in my friend's bedroom.

When I looked for food in the kitchen, I found a baguette and some pâté. The baguette was the thinnest bread stick I'd ever seen; its diameter was that of a U.S. quarter coin. Moreover, the pâté came in the smallest tin I'd ever seen. Undeterred, I popped the top and dug at the pâté with a spoon, then spread it on a disk of bread.

•

There was a young woman staying in the same place. I didn't know what she was doing there. When I first saw her, she was watching a television show — the characters were college students who kept losing their pants and falling down.

One time, my friend played a game with the young woman. He lay on his back, held her arms and pushed against her stomach with his feet, so her body was balanced over him. Then he laid her on her back and knelt between her legs. He put his hands behind her knees and lifted her pelvis toward him. They stayed that way for a while, rocking.

•

I thought Paris was small, but actually only the amount of ground I covered was small. I would walk from one point to another and think that I'd gone from one side of the city to the other. The reality was, I'd passed only from one district to another.

The place I visited most often was the adult strip of the Rue Saint-Denis. The shops there showed films that played continuously. If you stayed past the end, the clip would loop back to the beginning. The effect was one of perpetual sexual activity.

I found an aggressive vignette featuring a black-haired woman wearing leather boots and a headband. I was convinced she was a Native American. I imagined that she'd been separated from her tribe. Off the reservation, she was confined to a small room, with only a sawhorse as furniture. This was not her lucky day.

The problem was, the film was only about ten minutes long, so the repetition soon grew tiresome. After the third loop, I couldn't watch another round of brutal activity.

•

I went back to where I was staying. The baguette and pâté had been eaten, so my friend and I went to a restaurant. The problem was, we couldn't read the menu. We guessed at a selection and ended up with a plate of snails, which were not bad, not at all. They had obviously just been harvested from a damp lawn. I could taste the dew.

Later, we found a better place to eat: a cafeteria. The food there was plentiful, varied and cheap. In addition, the place was located near the Rue Saint-Denis — a big plus, in my opinion.

At one point, as we sat there, my friend asked me for some coins. "I need them to open the stall in the men's room," he explained. "There's some action back there."

"What do you mean by 'action'?" I asked.

"A man met my eyes with his eyes. You know what that means. Do you have any change?"

"How much?"

"Two francs."

That was about 50 cents. I gave him the coins. I didn't mind. I was off to the Rue Saint-Denis.

●

Another time, my friend and I were sitting in the apartment with the main tenant, the commercial director. The two of them were smoking a hashish-and-tobacco cigar and talking about someone they knew, Annie — her name was pronounced Ah-NEE.

"I spent the night with her," my friend said. "She scraped me with her nails, and I got an infection."

"She's a bitch," the director said, grinning.

I helped them finish the hash cigar, and all of us meditated on Annie.

●

Later, my friend and I went to visit Annie in her apartment across the river. Her place was luxurious, with a polished-wood floor and a grand piano. Through the large windows, we could see a park with trees and the Eiffel Tower.

Annie wasn't unfriendly or friendly. She just sat there with us. "There are two kinds of people," she told me, "intellectuals, and those who follow their instincts.

"I'm the second," she continued. "I can meet someone on a train, get off at the next station, have sex with him, and get back on the train."

- 113 -

"I followed her here," my friend explained to me. "She's the reason I'm in Paris."

Shortly, I left the apartment, but my friend stayed. I hoped Annie would not scrape him again with her nails.

●

When I finally took the subway, I noticed that the trains ran quietly. They didn't shriek with the sound of metal against metal. My friend told me that was because the trains had rubber wheels, and I believed him. I imagined the tracks were flat, and wide enough for tires to pass over. I didn't look closely as a train went by to see if it had steel wheels.

I took one of the trains to meet a French couple I knew from New York. But when I got to the address they had given me, they were not home. Someone I didn't know was there, but he was hospitable. He served me a greenish-yellow liqueur. I disliked the taste but drank it anyway. Unable to converse, I sat in the small, unfamiliar apartment for a long while, sipping at my glass of chartreuse, nodding occasionally at my host.

The couple I knew never showed up. After a time, I took a quiet train back to where I was staying.

●

Back at the storefront apartment, I got the young woman to sit while I drew her portrait. Her face filled a page of my sketchbook. I thought it was a perfect face, but on second glance, I could see its flaws. The mouth was too wide, the eyes too big. Those distortions, however, might have been due not to my model but to my own lack of skill.

At night, my friend brought out an envelope of drugs. "It's Paris-brand junk," he said. "It's stronger than what you get in New York."

I sniffed some of the powder and immediately felt sick. I ran to WC, but by the time I got there, the wave of nausea had passed. I returned to my friend's room and lay down. Again, I felt the sickness, so I got up and returned to the WC. I repeated this pattern for most of the night.

●

In the daytime, I went out walking. I still believed I could get anywhere I wanted on foot. I walked to the cathedral in the middle of the river. The structure had flying buttresses and craning gargoyles. The animals' heads stuck out on long necks, ready to spew boiling oil on anyone who approached.

I wanted to go into the cathedral, but a private event was being held. It was my last day in the city. I walked around the outside of the structure, looking at the buttresses and gargoyles, enjoying the flow of the river and my freedom from Paris-brand junk, then went back to where I was staying.

●

The next day, I had to take a train to another city. The train ran all night, and there were no seats, so I slept standing up. I leaned against a wall and dozed until my knees buckled. Before I fell over, I woke up. Then I leaned back and dozed again.

In a waking dream, I saw two women behind the glass door of a nearby compartment. They were sitting on opposite sides of a small table. One of them was holding a carrot with a Band-Aid wrapped around its middle. She pointed at the bandaged root, and her companion looked closely. The carrot was large and well wrapped. The companion gestured in turn at the erect carrot, and both women started to laugh uncontrollably. The first woman held the carrot over her head and waved it while both women covered their mouths with their hands.

As the train proceeded, the names of towns changed. Mulhouse became Mulhausen, Bale became Basel, and la Suisse became Schweiz. At first, I really thought I was getting somewhere. I thought I was entering a different country. But soon enough, I realized I was still in France.

Michèle Rakotoson
SHE, IN SPRINGTIME:
Selection

— Translated by Allison M. Charette

The Ravoajas lived in a group of six- and seven-story buildings grouped around a bare patch of lawn where faded signs of former glory stated, *WALKING ON GRASS PROHIBITED.*

The buildings were covered in a uniform layer of yellow and red paint. Orangey yellow — sad, dirty, like the skin of someone suffering from hepatitis — with red windows and doors, concentrated hemoglobin, it didn't help the overall look.

Deep discomfort washed over Sahondra. How did you get into the buildings? They certainly weren't made for being lived in, and they definitely shouldn't have been, besides. Something was missing, missing ...

It took her a few seconds to realize that the most oppressive thing in the place was the silence, and not the silence of the countryside and open spaces like at home, a silence where you could feel the earth as it breathed in and out. No, this was a deep silence, a defiant silence, a silence of death and absence. Of course she could hear sounds of the city a little further away, the cars, and the metro farther still, but that was just motors, superficial noises that would wear you down when you weren't paying attention. They weren't sounds from humans, children playing in the street, animals squawking, wind, running water, women calling out to each other, talking loudly, or even arguing, the pounding radio, men whistling. It wasn't the sound of pots cooking at ten in the morning, sounds escaping from the kitchen, the debates of men who were changing the world from inside their half-empty bottles, street vendors hawking their wares at the markets. It was utter emptiness.

Nothing came through the half-closed shutters, nothing could be seen of what was happening behind the curtains, because not only were the windows all closed, but the thick fabric made them even more opaque. Nothing breathed. No life.

A young couple passed by. Two people in jeans and black leather jackets, both strikingly asexual, him with his longish hair and soft cheekbones, her with her wifebeater and biker boots.

"I'm looking for Building C."

"Right behind you. Do you have the code to get in?"

"The what?"

"The number for the code, they just set it up. But you can try anyway, I mean, sometimes they leave it open during the day."

They left with a half-smile, and she stood in front of a closed door, shut tight, hermetically sealed.

Ridiculous, absolutely ridiculous. Not only did they make glass doors that gave the illusion that there was no door, but some of them opened by themselves and others just refused to open, and how were you supposed to make this damned thingy move, it was just stubbornly staying closed, there wasn't even a handle or a —

"You have to press the door button."

"The door button? What door button?"

"The one on the number pad."

And there it was again, that number pad just to get into a house.

"Come on, follow me."

A woman had arrived with a rolling cart of groceries. She'd glanced quickly at Sahondra, eyed her suitcase, hurried into the elevator, and asked curtly, "What floor?"

Then she looked again at distraught, confused Sahondra, and asked her, more kindly, "Have you just arrived? Is this your first time here?"

And without listening to her reply, the woman read Sahondra's sheet of paper and said, "They live on the seventh floor on the left," before getting out of the elevator with a quick, "Good bye, mademoiselle."

The seventh floor was a dark hallway, and Sahondra groped around it for a few seconds, because she figured that there had to be some sort of button somewhere, because everything in this country worked by pushing a button. Her hands fumbled across the wall until she saw a small glowing rectangle, which she pressed. In the bright hallway, she looked for a doorbell. A young man opened the door.

She dove right in without taking a breath: "I'm Randria's cousin."

The teenager was taken aback.

She had to risk it: "I just arrived, and I don't know where to go."

His mouth was still hanging open.

Tears came, which she tried desperately to contain. "I just got here …"

Weep for me, oh Lord, weep and make this young man pity me.

He seemed nice. He looked dazed, but finally muttered, "My mother isn't here right now, she makes the decisions around here. But look, you can stay here, my brother doesn't have class today, you can talk to Véro when she gets back."

She stared at him.

"Véro's my mom, she's working and won't be back until tonight, and I have to go to school now."

Silence.

"Uh, I don't know what else to tell you, all you have to do is go in, Pierre-Louis' in there, maybe he can give you his keys."

And without pressuring her either way, he started back inside, and she followed, not really knowing what to do, either.

"Are you thirsty? Would you like a glass of juice? Pierre-Louis!"

Pierre-Louis was a bit younger, around fourteen. He yawned and grumbled a quick "hey".

"Pierre-Louis, I have to go, she just got here, she doesn't know anyone in Paris, can you take care of her? I have to leave. Véro won't be back until tonight."

Pierre-Louis mumbled something, then looked at her and walked off into the kitchen, coming back with a large glass of juice, which he set directly in front of her.

"Or d'you like grapefruit juice better?"

And he turned on the stereo, not listening to her reply, either.

"What kind of music d'you like? I'm good with rock, I've got a hard rock CD if you want, I used to really like the group 'La souris déglinguée,' but I like rap better now. D'you know what rap is?"

She managed to swallow before saying good Lord, no, she didn't know what rap was, and under the teenager's pitying look she felt old, so old.

"It's okay, you're just like Véro, she doesn't know anything about pop culture, she pretends to, but … "

The Véro in question was his mother, of course. Pierre-Louis talked and talked, filling the silence with both questions and answers. He'd taken the young woman under his protection, she seemed so lost, and besides, wasn't he himself also a Malagasy? He'd never seen the country, and she came from there, but he couldn't bring himself to ask her what it was like, young men of fourteen have their dignity, but when a Malagasy woman came from so far away and she didn't know anything about France, it was his responsibility, as a gallant knight, to usher her into his universe.

"D'you like hamburgers?"

"Ham what?"

She was an idiot. Definitely an idiot.

"Uh, hamburgers. Fast food. There's a place around the corner, I'm meeting some friends there, you'll see, it's a blast, you can come if you want, you'll see, it's superfun."

"What does a blast mean?"

"You can't have a blast in Madagascar? I dunno. It's something that's cool, or like when you laugh your head off. Or just have a good time. Don't you ever have an awesome night in Madagascar? My cousin says that there's rock music down there."

"Yes, we have rock in Madagascar, and one time, a lot of the youth were mad and they flipped a bus over."

"Flipped a bus? Wow, that must've made the other guy pissed."

"What other guy?"

"Uh, the president, right? We've got concerts here, with Tonton, stuff like that, sometimes it's scary 'cause there's skinheads, and the nouveau poor, and Tonton's not really comfy with it, but I dunno, that's just what Véro said."

France was truly another planet, and Pierre-Louis' universe very far from her own. In high school, she'd learned the subjunctive and pluperfect and all the other verb tenses, and subject-verb-object sentences, but if she didn't go with Pierre-Louis, what would she do all day in that apartment?

Which was actually very nice: there were posters all over the walls, and flowers, and throw pillows. In the kitchen, there were appliances, lots of them, a refrigerator, a gas stove, and other machines. A senior official's residence. Véro had to be very rich. But Sahondra, what was she doing there, anyway? Grandmother would have disapproved. *Aren't you ashamed of just turning up at people's houses like this?* Yes, of course, but there hadn't been anyone there to welcome her.

"Come on, let's go outside," Pierre-Louis said kindly, seeing her on the verge of tears again. "And if you want, I'll give you a copy of the keys, so you can walk around by yourself, and tonight, you can sleep in my room, I'll tell Véro you're going to. There's a lot of us here, we've got cousins staying in the apartment, but it's cool, you'll be with me."

He casually took charge of her and kept her with him all day, carefully explaining everything like it was nothing: what she had to do to take the metro, how to buy her tickets, the various ticket categories, how to use the maps, how to make a phone call with a card or with coins, pointing out the various metro stations that she'd be using most often, and essentially introducing this woman into his world, the girl who came from a country that was also his and that he knew nothing about.

●

"Did you sleep well?"

The voice was pleasant. The apartment was bright, clean, almost empty: the mattresses had been put away, the couch folded back up, the cupboards closed, the occupants gone, with not a even single comforter left lying around, no forgotten sheets. It was like she'd been dreaming, or like the twelve people who'd been living there the day before had vanished into thin air. But they had been there. All of them. There'd been four of them sleeping in each ten-square-meter bedroom, cousins of cousins. But now, this morning, there was breakfast laid out. Milk, hot chocolate, butter, jam, bread, even juice. Just for the two of them.

"What would you like to eat? Fruit, eggs? Have to eat well here, in the morning, because the food in the lunchroom isn't very nutritious. Me, with the boys here, you know, I always have to make sure that they're eating properly. They eat so badly away from home, I really like them to leave with a full stomach."

Surely she must have meant a luxuriously stuffed stomach. But Véro had already set food in front of her. Bread with butter and jam, milk, hot chocolate, a glass of juice ... And what was simmering in those enormous pots? No time to ask, though. Véro made her gulp everything down, tiny Véro, who was shorter than she was and who looked like the boys' younger sister.

The apartment was empty, and the hot chocolate silky, like in the movies.

"They've all left already. Some of them work far away, and besides, it's better, during the day, if there aren't too many of us here, I'd really prefer not to have to explain it to the super, if he stops by."

"If he what?"

"The apartment is supposed to house four people. And if any of our relatives ever needs proof of address, we have to fall within regulations."

Because the laws are that strict in Paris?

"So, what are you going to do?"

"I don't know. I have a cousin in Rouen, and another in Bourg-en-Bresse ... "

"Are you sure of their address?"

Sure? How could she be sure of anything right now?

"Why did you come here, then? You've got to start taking care of your stipend today."

But how was she supposed to take care of the stipend? Véro is the type of person who gives orders and demands answers.

"Louis is working this morning, you'll have to go by yourself. Here's a map of the metro and a set of house keys. You'll see, it's easy to get home, you've seen the metro station, otherwise, there's the 78 bus that stops right over there. If you have any problems, call."

Her hostess' voice was firm — she had decided. Sahondra was like her little sister, she was taking responsibility for the girl. And she only came up to her son's shoulder.

"After that, you can take care of finding yourself an apartment."

Her tone was a little harsh. Faced with Sahondra's terrified expression, she softened a little.

"I'm sorry to be so rough on you," she said, "but there's nothing else I can do. This is a small apartment, and there are too many of us here, I can't take care of so many people."

Véro really couldn't do more. Sahondra understood perfectly well. The apartment wasn't empty, like she'd thought when she woke up. There were already twelve of them there. The night before, Véro's husband had been the first to come home. He was still a young man, smiling and quiet. Then, Guy, the oldest son, came; then, a cousin who'd just made it in and hadn't found a room in the city yet; then another couple, friends or cousins, who'd been out on the street, someone had explained.

So twelve of them were there. Well, thirteen, with Sahondra, thirteen in seventy square meters, like at home. And like at home, the lady of the house — Véro, in this instance — had laid out a plan for the space, without leaving her kitchen.

"Guy, clear a space in your room for her, she'll be sleeping here tonight, we'll figure out what we can do for her afterward. Naivo and Rija, open up the couch. Pierre-Louis, you — "

But Pierre-Louis had interrupted, protesting forcefully, "Oh come on, I already worked my a** off and made up a bed for her, you only had to say something."

It was impudent, but instead of smacking him across the face like any Malagasy mother would have done, Véro had just said, "Well, in that case, open a window to air out your room, and throw your porno magazines in the closet, she doesn't have to care for the same literature as you do. And make up another mattress, Tiana's also going to be sleeping there."

Her husband hadn't said a word, his nose in his newspaper, contributing nothing to the conversation.

•

"Oh, my child," Grandmother had said one day, when she learned, God knows how, that there was a train that ran underground in France, "oh, my child, white men are mad. They spend their time playing with the devil. You'll see, one day, they'll find themselves face-to-face with Satan. I've heard they even want to make a train run under the ocean. One of these days, the elements will rise up against them. Man should never trespass like that into the realm of the dead. I hope that if you ever go there one day, you'll refuse to go underground."

Sadly, Grandmother, Sahondra disobeyed. She went underground, into the stupid tunnel they call a metro. Got lost there, of course. And yes, white people are mad, but they're also sadistic. You'd have to have one hell of an imagination to create the damned thingy, this maze of interlacing tunnels, hallways, and labyrinthine corridors, where every breath seems to require supernatural effort, where you travel by lamps run on electricity or something that makes you look pale and haggard, where you have to fall in running behind men and women who make a point not to look at you. Sure, there were singers or musicians here and there to try and lift the mood in that surreal, murky world, but a guitar in the metro makes the most sorrowful sounds in the world.

And you have to orient yourself inside there, somehow. Véro had given her a piece of paper with the station names written on it: Vavin, Pigalle, Crimée, Saint-Augustin, Barbès, Château Rouge … But Grandmother was most certainly right, Sahondra was lost underground, completely lost.

She's going to cry, she's going to cry … a train underground … and everyone ignores her, she takes a deep breath, looks at the map, tries to put on a brave face. She got on the metro at Jeanne d'Arc, now she has to go to Vavin, and then …

Oh, bravo, Sahondra, you made it! She made it out of the metro safe and sound!

Finally, the open air. And something strange.

She can't find her bearings, not at all. No north, no south, even the sun looks like it's in the wrong place.

And she has to find where she's going. Or maybe first just orient herself in this mess. Or try asking someone.

"Excuse me, Monsieur … okay, next one … Monsieur … " What's wrong with this country? Finally, someone who looks nice.

"Sorry-I-don't-speak-French."

Sure, it's true that Africans have become Francophone, Anglophone, and Lusophone, and that their mother tongues are now vernacular languages, but … fine, no comment here.

"Madame, please."

Whew, this one answers her, and even kindly. "Oh, that's easy. Turn right, then turn left, take the alley east, then stay to the right."

Easy? This lady's worse than an Antandroy, and they're so used to their deserted region that when they say "It's not far from here," you'd better be ready to walk for the whole afternoon.

But Sahondra turns right, then left, then takes the alley east, and finds herself in front of the building she was looking for: the place that houses the office that handles stipends.

It's 11 a.m. It took her three hours to find her bearings in the metro. Three hours.

It's a tall, red-brick structure with a glass door. Very austere. But nothing scares Sahondra anymore, she's starting to get used to this, she quickly finds the button to get inside, and almost as quickly finds the little sign that says, "Buzz and push." She buzzes, then pushes, and finds herself in an empty lobby.

And since Paris has almost no secrets for her anymore, she looks for either an information desk or a sign.

Found it! "Stipend Office, second floor." There's even an arrow pointing to the staircase, which she climbs. Though her knees are shaking slightly. This is the place that will decide her future, which will allow her, among other things, to attend university in France.

Fear hatches a pulsing kind of energy that smashes her shyness to smithereens. She manages to make her way through one door. That leads to a dark corridor and other closed doors, and she manages to knock on another door, explain her issue without stammering too much, she even manages to speak without wondering if her French is correct or not, show all the papers she has on her, all the letters, requests, everything.

"Wait here, we'll see," she's told.

She goes to sit down in a waiting room, and waits for a long time, a very long time. It's a quarter to one when it's her turn, and they said offices close at 1 o' clock, and there's only two of them left there. The other person is a huge African man, very sharply dressed, and his wife just left in frustration, she was wearing a wonderful wrap, clasps, and jewelry. Before them, there had been other students, poorer students, anxious as she is, one of them had talked for a long time, about his country, Lebanon, about his desperate flight, and everyone else had listened, without saying much. Where did they all come from?

Now she was alone in the waiting room, alone before the closed doors, empty offices. What if no one came to call her? What if no one helped her? At 1 o' clock, everything closes. What could they be talking about? What? It was five 'til one, she could hear raised voices, it'd been almost ten minutes that the other man had been in there, the shouting got louder.

The student's the one screaming! "Madame, this is supposed to be a doctorate stipend, a research stipend, the amount that you're giving me is ridiculous!"

He dares to raise his voice! It's 1 p.m. The man leaves, furious.

Her meeting goes faster. It's likely that she'll receive a stipend, but the Malagasy government hasn't replied yet, there's a letter missing, an important one, the approval letter, and without that letter …

But it's 1:10, the woman behind the desk looks tired, Sahondra doesn't know what to do anymore, it looks like everything's going to be smashed to smithereens.

"Come back in ten days, maybe the missing letter will have arrived by then."

The young woman is clearly ready for her break. How many files has she processed today? But Sahondra falls apart, dissolving into sobs, hiccups, and despair.

"My mother sold our rice fields," she says, "no one came to meet me here, and Véro doesn't want me around."

There are no logical explanations, no chance of hope, she's going to get lost in Paris, die in Paris.

"Look, I'll send a telex, and you should ask around on your end, you should call someone in your family so they can go ask the ministry or something. At any rate, it'll just be a few days, you're not on the streets right now."

She even goes so far as to offer her a glass of water, then guides Sahondra kindly to the door, who overhears her say to her colleague, "The files didn't come in, the poor girl came here with nothing. They really have to start some awareness campaign, warn future candidates so that they don't just venture into France like that, setting off on some adventure. It can be a disaster."

Another voice, lower, sharper, replies, "You know that they'll come anyway, whether we warn them or not."

The door closed again, the voices trailed off, Paris lay before her, and anger again, too. Who dared to say that she was a disaster? All she had left was the advice of another student, pragmatic, who told her to go to the university, the embassy, anywhere, so as not to surrender to despair. She took a few steps to control her fear, to get used to Paris, and decided to go straight back to the apartment to write home, and figure out her enrollment at school, and get her residency forms in order.

•

It was like déjà vu of sounds and feelings: heels click-clacking across dozens of kilometers of Parisian asphalt, eyes becoming accustomed to looking not at anyone else, but straight ahead. She learned to live in Paris. Slowly.

She couldn't tell if she was making progress or losing ground in her odyssey. She had found her bearings, her landmarks: Véro's apartment, the corner newsstand, the metro, the path that she changes a little from time to time in order to understand the city better. Her spirits started fading, slowly being replaced by fear and dread, sadness, nostalgia, maybe because of the colder days approaching. And because of the surprises from time to time, like the day she went to enroll at the university.

The university. Dirty, haphazard buildings, covered in graffiti, with dusty stairwells. It was mid-September, the courtyard was empty. The students away. And her father's dream, where had it hidden? He talked about it so much, he could already see the moment when his daughter would come home with her degree, he boasted about how wise and influential she would be, he listed everyone who'd be jealous, while her mother, in addition to the list of young men who might deserve her daughter's hand, made a list of the presents to bring back for everyone. "Don't forget to write your aunt, your uncle, our neighbors, my girlfriend, your cousins. Our only wealth is in our family and friends, and if you don't help anyone, no one else will ever come to help you, and don't forget to write, don't you dare forget."

And what would she have to tell her parents now? That the buildings were dilapidated, that the air was cold? That by some measures, the university in France looked like the one in Antananarivo? But who would believe her? There was a myth that failure did not exist in France, neither failure nor misery. If the available Paradise wasn't actually paradise, where could anyone go to find something to ease their despair? She sighed: anyway, whatever happened, for now, she had to get enrolled.

The building was cylindrical, the hallway spun around, and so did Sahondra. She got dizzy, knocking at door after door, the rooms all locked, or empty.

She'd been followed by a persistent smell for a bit. Someone must have stepped in dog poop. There were weird smells lingering in that hallway and no air circulation, but surely a dog couldn't have gotten that far in to go. She was all the way up on the 4th floor, a 4th floor of broken elevators and dark stairwells. What animal would have ventured up there … or what if it was her? She looked at the sole of her shoe and retched.

"Who are you looking for?"

A young man in jeans and a leather jacket was smiling at her. For a moment, she thought they knew each other, she'd seen the jeans and leather jacket before, Guy wore the same ones, but no, that was probably the fashion, all the twenty-somethings in France wore the same things. But this young man had lighter skin and wavy hair, an Arab.

"No point trying so hard right now, nobody's here, it's still break, you won't find anyone around. Come back next week, there's no hurry, they still have to prep for the second term. Did you preregister?"

Of course she preregistered, how could she get into France without preregistering? She was probably even going to have a stipend. She'd done everything she had to, everything. She hadn't come all this way for nothing.

"If you've preregistered, you're fine. Otherwise, you'd need to buckle down on Monday morning. Go to 304, the woman there is extremely competent, she'll point you toward a nice professor. What are you studying for?"

"A bachelor's."

"Okay, yeah, you've got time. Don't get them all worked up, though, they're usually in a bad mood when they get back from break."

But she had to do something in the meantime, she couldn't just wait around.

"Go to the sixth floor, they've got all the forms up there, you can register for your diploma already, or get your residency card or permit or whatever figured out, or your guarantor papers, or something."

Guarantor papers?

The young man walked away with a "good luck".

On the sixth floor, there was a note written in marker: *Closed — back on Monday, September 24.*

Paris was so very gray, gray enough to make her cry. She'd never expected this kind of welcome. She had to figure it out by herself, she didn't know what to do, where to go, people gave her unspecific advice, and then whatever happened, happened. If only people in the street would smile at her, even a little. But no, each one acted as if he were the most highly preoccupied person, and they all ran around without looking at each other, stuffed into oversized sweaters, mufflers, and dark colors.

Then, just before hitting rock bottom, Sahondra decided that she was going to conquer Paris and its academic laurels, that she would achieve her father's dream, she would walk down the Champs-Elysées all dressed in white, and better yet, she would invite her old man to join her, so that he could share in her success —

A car raced by, interrupting her musings, a hand pulling her back by the shoulder.

"Are you alright, sister?"

It was a young African man, a helmet wedged onto the crown of his head.

"You have to look both ways before you cross the street."

He was almost smiling, even looked friendly.

"Did you just get here? What country are you from?"

Sahondra just stared at him, lost, so he shrugged his shoulders, the light turned green, and she barely had time to sigh before the young man was already long gone.

•

Sahondra moved in officially with Véro while she waited. She had dedicated herself to exile in the same way as someone dedicating themselves to religion or writing. It was a waltz in three: two steps forward, one step back, one step forward, two steps back, spin around, and the faint music, so faint, light like the papers that she was asked for everywhere for a waltz that she hadn't expected. It was becoming more and more difficult. "Come back later," everyone repeated, "come back later." But why? She couldn't get a residency card without being enrolled in the university, no enrollment without a residency card, and that also required the guarantor papers stating that she had enough money to support herself, but how could she support herself without a working permit? And as for the stipend ... they had promised her that stipend. So why did the woman who had seen her the first time now look annoyed when she saw her come in? And she eventually just said, "Look, there's no use in you wasting time coming here. I'll let you know as soon as I hear anything."

Smile, good lady, smile and arch your back, leave tango to the slums and jazz to the junkies, and learn to slide along, let yourself be carried along on the surface of things and emotions, far from pain, play out your ills and make beautiful music of them, and smile, good lady, smile, even if it hurts ... especially if it hurts.

Sometimes, she reasoned that she was becoming a stoic and very patient saint, because sometimes it hurt, sometimes it hurt a lot. Like the day when she had to go to the police commissioner's office to get the residency card that she deserved.

She'd arrived very early that morning, following the advice she'd gotten from Véro's entire family. They'd reviewed all her papers, checked and rechecked everything to make sure she hadn't forgotten anything, and they'd showered her with recommendations.

"Don't speak too loudly, but don't let yourself get intimidated, you'll see, they're awful people, but if you're polite and insistent, everything will be fine, just make sure you hurry so you don't get there late."

She wasn't late, but neither was she the first one there, there were already fifty people waiting in silence for the doors to open, resigned, ready for the slaughter.

"This does not fall within regulations."

Heart stops beating, saliva evaporates, throat constricts ... smile ... the woman glares down at her sternly, oh God it's just her luck, everyone had warned her to avoid this woman, but she'd been given a number, and —

"I repeat, mademoiselle, you are here under fraudulent pretenses. You don't have the right to cross into French borders like this."

The woman was enormous, flushed pink, with a blouse that was pink too, stuck to her chest, which was itself quite ample.

Calm down, calm down, don't panic. The woman raised her voice.

"And what's your guarantor?"

Sahondra showed her the papers that Véro had prepped.

"Who's this?"

"A cousin."

"Sure. With you people ... And what about your proof of address?"

It was there, Jacquie had thought of everything, even a visit from a clerk in a police uniform.

The woman in pink muttered, "A cousin ... " She flipped through the paperwork again and spat sourly, "Nothing doing, this doesn't fall within regulations, you need a different visa, you can't study in France with this one."

Fortunately for Sahondra, she'd learned the ropes in Madagascar, she knew this kind of desk worker very well. Except back there, you could always slip a few coins over to mollify a power-crazed desk worker. Here, it was unthinkable, at least when done that obviously.

"I'm sorry, madame, but as you can see, I have a stipend, I have a place to live, I have all the necessary paperwork — "

"Yes, but not the visa!"

Even worse, this delightful woman was unyielding. Smile, Sahondra, smile.

"But at the French Embassy in Madagascar, they said that … " Keep smiling, Sahondra, smile. Some people, she found out later, had paid 10,000 francs to embassy clerks for the wrong visa. How could you keep smiling at that? It had been so many days that she'd smiled to keep from screaming. The charming woman's right nostril was crowned with a dark red wart that rose and fell as she breathed, which was the only thing that saved Sahondra, saving her sense of humor, and more importantly, giving her the courage to play her trump card.

"If you'd like a form guaranteeing that I'm enrolled somewhere, madame, I can come back with a signature from my advisor at the university."

Suspicion flickered through the eyes of the Amazonian woman. To her, Sahondra clearly seemed too sweet to be honest.

"What are you going to be studying?"

"Journalism, madame, at the Center for Journalistic Development."

"Because you're a journalist?"

"Yes, madame."

This time, the woman's chin rose endearingly toward the curve of her nose.

"Juliette — " (Juliette had to be the director, she was wearing a tailored suit) " — this young woman says she's a journalist."

In some situations, any face is suspicious by default, but Sahondra, she had one of the most angelic smiles around, she was willing to play the Marseillaise on a hunting bugle across all of Paris if they wanted her to, if only to get the prized visa.

"Yes madame, my advisor said that if I needed a paper or anything … " Thank you, Guy, thank you. He'd told her about a Turkish friend who'd managed to recover his papers from within the clutches of a similar harpy. *Try it anyway*, he'd whispered, *say you're a journalist*.

But it looked like that hadn't wrapped anything up. The director was still thumbing through the forms, glancing up at Sahondra every so often, who smiled genially, trying to hide her trembling limbs. Lord, please don't let her ask for a form, please. But the director did seem a little more receptive to the young woman's distress. She even tried on her own half-smile.

"Alright, give her a three-month provisory visa, she should have one, at any rate. She'll need to come back, we'll figure that out later."

Later? She had three months in front of her to learn how to live in France, to get out or to sink into it like quicksand. And like any good Merina, Sahondra was endowed with incredible doggedness. She only had to arm herself with patience. For now, she was safe. She left the police commissioner's office with her sheet of paper, the sheet of paper that would let her stay in France and hopefully complete her studies. She looked at it lovingly, then set it very carefully into her purse.

•

Days had passed. She'd been there for eight weeks, brooding, and discouragement had crept up on her slowly. Everything was so much more difficult than she'd expected, it sometimes seemed like she was sinking into a bog or trying to move mountains at every turn. That was perhaps the feeling that frightened her the most: being useless, being someone's charge, not knowing what to do with herself. Sahondra tried to make herself invisible, helping around the house and fading into the woodwork. She was becoming irreversibly numb. What else could she do? It hadn't been that long since she'd thought of dancing on the crest of a wave, but her tightrope walker's body eventually started to toughen with the stress of tensing up to avoid falling, and the sea doesn't saturate the insides of a person.

While waiting for the promised stipend, she learned how to set aside her emotions and feelings. Days slid into each other, an insidious process of letters from her home country that didn't come and a gap that kept widening everywhere, in everything, in the entire country, in the concept of time, in every conversation she had.

Fortunately for her, courses at the university started up quickly. She began to learn about presumption and disdain there, from Cécilia. And other things, too: cafés, and long, nearly pointless debates on how to change the world.

The first time Sahondra had seen her, Cécilia asked, "What country are you from?" It was mid-October, the professor was droning on, "All transferences of technology or intelligence that have been enacted in the last twenty-five years … "

Sahondra was taking stacks of notes. Her neighbor snickered.

"Oh, come on. You know all that. That s*** is the reason you're here." And she fished out her nail polish and manicure set.

A beam of sunlight shone down into the lecture hall. A thin, tenacious beam that lit up a white girl. For an instant, Sahondra let herself imagine that she was elsewhere, back at home, in Madagascar. The teacher continued his lesson, without bothering to see if he was being listened to. Some people were listening, others yawned more or less discreetly, the place was overcrowded, outside it was starting to turn cold. And doubt came to her: what if her neighbor was right?

"Don't tell me you're actually sucked in by that pretty talk," she whispered. "You know all of this, everything they're saying, you've lived it. He's just wrapping it all up in words that sound nice, he's explaining to you why you and your country have such bad luck. You can't let yourself get shoved around like that, the main thing here is gonna be getting the bibliography, everything else will come automatically. But watch out though, you actually have to show up. They say that some Boards of Ed do attendance checks, the police commissioners actually require it."

Never had her nostalgia for her home sky been so strong. Nor had fear. After the days spent wandering around looking for God knows what — forms, guarantors, certificates — the university was her refuge, the reason for being there, the reason to keep going, definitely not a reason to be sent out of France.

She looked at Cécilia and wanted to tell her about the day when soldiers suppressed a protest, and a young man next to her had fallen with a bullet in his head. He was seventeen. No one knew his name, failed revolutions never have heroes, they just have mad *desperados*. She wanted to tell the story to Cécilia, but shut her lips discreetly and dove back into her note-taking, so as not to get depressed.

And now, tonight, here she was, surrounded by music boring into her eardrums, a bluish cigarette halo with a more-than-aggressive stench, androgynous faces melting into the same shadows, faded jeans and mass-produced leather jackets, voices that shouted to be heard and argued that the future of the world would depend on prison reform, genetic manipulation, or quantum mathematics. A waiter in a white shirt whirled between bags, benches, and lounging legs in a dangerous dance. At the bar, the cashier counted his money, accentuating his motions with "one express, one express".

These days, Sahondra always had the same nightmare: she was taking the Bac exam, the oral component, and right when she was about to speak, she looked up to see that the room was empty, the examiner had left, he'd forgotten her.

Cécilia lit a cigarette.

"Why'd you decide to come to France?"

Why choose France? To study, to get a degree, to obey her parents, to travel … or to remember her colonizers?

"I don't know, it seemed so obvious to come study here."

As obvious as the school of her childhood and adolescence, the school where she'd spent fifteen years of her life, as obvious as the little girls in gray and beige smocks, in tight rows and straight braids. "Ring around the rosey," they'd sing, "pocket full of posey, ashes, ashes, we all fall down."

Next to her, Cécilia cracked a smile and asked, "So, where are you with your papers?"

"They gave me a voucher good for three months, and then I'll have to start the process over again."

Cécilia had lost her whole family in the upheaval in her home country of Argentina, and she could only stay in France as a student.

Two musicians walked into the café, talked to the owner, and settled down in the corner. They started singing and the room fell quiet, the music swelled. For a second, Sahondra thought that one of them was smiling at her, she wanted to go up to him and tell him about Madagascar and Antananarivo, jazz musicians hadn't yet fled Antananarivo. But she just smiled back at him and hummed along.

Summertime …

The waiter came back with their orders. Steins of golden brown beer, where bubbles danced underneath the foam, such light foam.

"Dray re ry lanitra ô, mitonantonanana ny zanakao Rangahy ô, misotro toada ao amin'ny bara hono izy!" her father would have said if he'd seen her. "Sweet baby Jesus, what's happened to our daughter, is she drinking alcohol at a bar?!"

In Antananarivo, it must be said, there were only three of them, cafés that is: the one reserved for Western service workers, essentially on the fringes, single and alone with their temporary and fleeting companions, the more or less young prostitutes or low-bred women, trying their luck to avoid becoming an old whore who'd preside over one of the more sordid neighborhoods in a city in one of the poorest countries in the Third World. The second, more luxurious, was on the Place de la Présidence, the girls were prettier and still dreamt of love, while the French experts and Malagasy managers, all trussed up in their three-piece suits and gripping their briefcases tightly, pretended that AIDS doesn't exist in Madagascar. And then there were the bars, where …

Sahondra, in Paris, she had gotten used to the cafés, and blatantly ignored her memory, a friend who had said, one day, talking about young girls in bars, "Yeah whatever, they all dream of a handsome Apollo who will pull them out of their misery, and the ones who do scrounge up a ticket to elsewhere will end up stuck in the projects outside the city, spending their lives working as a temp cashier in the nearest chain store, and the ones who miss the boat will end up at the abattoir on Rue Saint-Denis, or possibly in a brothel in Abu Dhabi, but there, they prefer blondes, although there's always the possibility of being a croupier in Gabon."

Cécilia started talking absentmindedly, looking nowhere: "I always dreamt of living in Paris. Back home, people talked about the city of lights, about concerts and libraries and the Seine. I wanted to see Proust's country, but I'd forgotten that he died a long time ago, and I got here too late, they say I'm a political refugee."

How old was she? What can anyone do when the military takes power and turns crazy? The beer stein was slowly emptying of its golden liquid, the first swallows were bitter, so bitter, then Sahondra felt its warmth spreading through her body, her fears dissolving and a smile returning to her face.

Apparently, Cécilia had left Argentina under tragic circumstances, but she never talked about it.

The saxophonist was playing a little mechanically, his thoughts on something else. It was almost 11 at night, she was going to miss the last metro, she felt weary. They had wandered from café to café, and they were beginning to feel the alcohol and frustration. Sahondra had followed Cécilia to stay warm, to feel less alone. She would have loved to hear the stories about Bolivia, Argentina, and Chile, but Cécilia stayed mute, and the beer-induced haze flowed over her, leaving her nauseous.

In a corner, a tipsy man was singing.

Every day, I have the blues …

Almost to herself, Cécilia said, "Don't panic, there's no point. There's always an answer."

And she smiled reassuringly, adding, "Don't ever panic. For now, if you need money, I can lend you some."

When Sahondra tried to thank her, she scoffed and cut her off. "Drop it. You'll make it up to me someday. You've got to learn how to do things on your own."

Then she huffed, "If where you're staying's too hard, you can come live with me, I'll have room in two weeks."

"Two weeks."

Sahondra knew nothing of winter. She expected a very long, very cold one.

Walter Cummins
THE BEAUTIES OF PARIS

As Taylor and his daughter, Ariel, emerged through the Nothing to Declare door into the Charles de Gaulle arrival hall, he saw the driver, a little man with a pointed face and a hat three sizes too big, holding a cardboard printed with his name. When Taylor said he had to get euros, the driver took their luggage and, in memorized English, asked Taylor to meet him at pickup area 8. Instead of staying with her father, Ariel followed the man, one step behind, like a child, even though she was a woman in her thirties. In line for the cash dispenser, Taylor watched the driver pull a suitcase with each hand, the top of his hat at a level with Ariel's shoulders.

Three American businessmen clustered at the machine, paying more attention to their conversion than the buttons they had to push. Taylor almost said something, fidgeting with the notion that his daughter might run off with the little man and leave him stranded. But he swallowed his impatience, knew he was upset because he and Ariel had been seated rows apart on the crowded flight. He couldn't remember their last real conversation, if there had ever really been one, and he had anticipated seven hours to ease the tension before they got to Paris.

Finally stuffing a thousand euros into his wallet, he saw the sign for area 8 and walked quickly toward it and found himself blocked by a thick crowd coming the other way. He tried to squirm through, but a young woman in an airport uniform stopped him, signaling that he couldn't go ahead. "What's happening?" he asked in English, and a voice behind him answered, "Something about a bomb scare."

"Wonderful," Taylor sighed. It was a mistake, a colossal mistake, coming to Paris, bringing Ariel, as if time in another city would fix things. And now, according to the news, French students were protesting some law about jobs. Had some of them planted explosives? He didn't know what to expect.

Taylor had booked the arrangements six weeks before, shortly after Ariel's mother, his ex-wife, died. Ariel had cared for her, moving back to the room of her childhood for the final months of dreadful pain. The trip was his sister's idea, almost a demand. "Your daughter needs a treat after what she's been through." "Even with me?" he had said. "Even with you," his sister had told him, tight-lipped.

Calling to make the offer, he expected Ariel to refuse, especially after many seconds of silence, but when she spoke, it was "Yes," just the one word. Taylor had responded quickly, "It will be good for you to get away." He could almost hear her nodding, and she had said, "I'd like to get away." He had hoped for more enthusiasm, then realized she was just as apprehensive about spending time with him as he was to be alone with her.

Outside the terminal at area 6, Taylor realized a path to 8 was clear. He saw Ariel standing beside a yellow van, tall and thin, stoop shouldered, her face long and narrow, like his. Ever since she had been a teenager, he sensed she blamed him for her face. Despite the resemblance, he felt he was looking at a stranger. He knew she saw him, but she didn't gesture. It was a young woman emerging from the passenger door who did, plump and little with close-cropped hair. Taylor assumed she was the driver's daughter. Two fathers, two daughters.

Once he was belted on the bench seat beside Ariel. The young woman turned to him. "We go now."

"What about the protests?" Taylor asked her. "Will we be able to get into the museums and monuments?"

When she gave him a blank look, he tried again using remnants of his college French: "Voulez nous visit les monuments y des musee? Avec les protester contre de law?"

She smiled and shook her head in bewilderment.

"Stop it," Ariel said, her voice sharp, the first time she had spoken since they got off the plane. "You're not making any sense."

"At least I'm amusing her. The stupid American she can talk about to friends."

When the van pulled off a highway onto a city street, Taylor craned for a street sign and took out his map. He liked tracing routes, hoping to find the way to their hotel. For several blocks he was lost, then located Faubourg St. Antoine in grids F26-27, a nondescript avenue that could have existed in a dozen cities. At first he was eager to show Ariel, but when he saw that she was staring straight at the driver's hat, said nothing.

With the turn onto Avenue Ledru Rollin, he knew exactly where they were, heading directly toward Pont d'Austerlitz to cross onto the Left Bank. But at the intersection with Rue de Lyon, a group of what looked like fourteen-year-olds, mostly boys, mostly dark skinned, swarmed over the street, blocking traffic, chanting and pumping their fists. The cars ahead of them turned away, but their driver — to Taylor's surprise — chose to go straight ahead. "What are you doing?" he said and could see Ariel cowering, hunched forward, her arms pressed tight across her chest.

The driver stopped when the children surrounded the van. Two boys with wool ski caps pulled down to their eyebrows suddenly slid back the door on Taylor's side, exposing him. They shouted something he did not understand, and he tensed, expecting them to pull him out onto the street. When they hesitated, he slammed the door closed, gripping the handle and leaning his weight into it.

Other boys popped open the driver's door and stuck their heads inside. The driver nodded and blew the horn, again and again. The children let out a cheer, backing off from the van and waving. They parted to let the driver creep through, slapping hands on the van's metal.

Taylor sat back, wiping sweat from his forehead with the sleeve of his jacket. "They're just kids," he said. "Playing at being protesters. Harmless." He hoped Ariel would nod, but her jaw was clenched.

When they crossed Pont d'Austerlitz, he pointed to the sign for the Jardin des Plantes and tried speaking to her again. "Remember when you were here as a little girl?" Twenty-four years ago, he quickly calculated. "You wanted to come back to the zoo every day we were in Paris. The lions and tigers fascinated you. The big cats."

"But we only went once."

"Your mother took you shopping instead."

"She still had some of the silk scarves she bought. In a drawer. I don't think she ever wore them."

"People are like that," Taylor said. "They consider some possessions too good to use."

"Then they die."

"Maybe actually wearing them would have been a disappointment." He didn't know why he said that.

"Mother had more than enough to disappoint her." Ariel almost whispered the words, as if she didn't want to be overheard by the driver and the young woman who might have been the man's daughter.

Before Taylor could think of a response, the van double-parked in front of their hotel, the driver jumping out to raise the back hatch and unload their suitcases onto the sidewalk. Taylor overtipped the little man, a twenty euro note, the smallest bill from the money machine, relieved to have gotten this far. With a "Merci, monsieur," the man was back in the van and gone, the vehicle vanished around a corner.

Taylor held the door so that Ariel could enter the small lobby first. Because he wanted to be on the Left Bank near quaint Rue Mouffetard and the cafes of Place de la Contrescarpe, he had found a web site that recommended this small three-star hotel on Rue Monge, a working class avenue lined with shops, a tiny plumbing supply store on one side of the hotel and a laundry on the other.

Once registered, they crowded their luggage into a narrow elevator up to rooms on the third floor. Ariel's was across from his, facing the street. When she unlocked the door, he saw how small her room was, barely enough space to maneuver around the bed to the wardrobe. "Do you want to take a nap?" he asked her.

"I'm exhausted. I need a shower."

He suggested they meet for dinner at seven, four hours away. He would call for her. She shut the door and bolted it. Taylor kicked off his shoes and stretched out on his own bed, his eyes burning, unable to sleep. His room seemed even smaller than his daughter's, the walls closing in. He turned on the TV and clicked through channels until he found BBC news, not paying attention until the screen showed pictures of the demonstrations in Paris, store windows smashed and a car smoldering on its side. But that was on the other side of the city, far away.

Taylor propped himself up on two pillows and tried to imagine how he would talk to his daughter, how to start a conversation. Ariel had been barely a teenager when he divorced her mother, off to college a few years later and then to a job several hundred miles from where he had ended up. While she was young, they saw each other only a few times a year when he drove hours for a meal in a restaurant, neutral territory, Ariel stealing glances at her watch, checking how long it would be before her mother came to get her. Taylor couldn't understand how his daughter could live with the woman, the way she had let herself go, the house a disaster. But he knew better than to criticize, asking meaningless questions about school, eager for signs of the infant he had been thrilled to hold.

During the period of his second marriage, they didn't have much contact, not after Ariel's initial reaction to Carolyn, only ten years older than her, an attractive woman whose manic need for entertainment eventually exhausted Taylor. He had never known the men in Ariel's life, not even the one named James during her brief engagement. Ariel hadn't been lucky with men. He remembered looking at her when she was an adolescent and realizing that she wasn't attractive. No one will love her, he told himself then, immediately guilty for the thought. Every time the memory came back to him, he felt ashamed.

Taylor had visited Paris a number of times since that first trip with Ariel and her mother, twice with Carolyn and later on his own, more fond of the city with each visit. He had hoped his adult daughter would fall in love with it too, the two of them sharing its treasures, their days filled with conversations about art and architecture, food and wine. A closeness would emerge. But now that he was here, shut into this room with a tiny window that overlooked a tar roof, he didn't know how to begin.

After an hour of staring at a framed poster on the wall, a famous one by an artist whose name he couldn't remember, Taylor gave up trying to sleep. He took a long hot shower and then shaved, wiping the steamed mirror with the edge of his hand again and again. But his reflection kept disappearing in a mist. Even in clean clothes he didn't feel refreshed. He sat on the edge of his bed, watching the minute hand of his travel alarm till it was exactly seven and he could knock on Ariel's door.

She wasn't hungry and didn't want a drink. "Airplane food?" he asked.

She nodded. "I don't have any appetite. It was a rotten flight. I felt cramped into that window seat."

"You've got long legs." Taylor regretted the words as soon as he spoke them. Her height was another thing she didn't like about herself, though for her generation it wasn't unusual. "I wish we could have sat together."

"I tried to sleep the whole flight."

"Did you?"

"Not at all." She shook her head.

"What about now?"

"It takes me a while to get used to a new bed."

Across Rue Monge, Taylor noticed a dual stairway leading up to Rue Rollin. "How do you feel about a climb?"

She shrugged. "You know this city."

His legs ached and he had to rub his thighs at the halfway landing. Ariel gave the hint of smile. It was the first time he had seen her amused. "I'm showing my age," he said.

After a quick right and then left, they came to Rue Descartes, a narrow street lined with restaurants. Taylor had eaten at several one or two trips ago, recalled the photos of celebrities on the white stone wall inside La Maison de Verlaine, on the ground floor of a building the poet had once lived in, and decades later, Hemingway. In the picture directly across from his table, Jack and Jackie Kennedy and Lyndon and Lady Bird Johnson stood together smiling at the camera. Bang, he had kept thinking. Bang, you're dead.

At the corner of Rue Clovis, Taylor recognized the dome of the Pantheon illuminated by spotlights. Groups of students walked on both sides of the street, chatting happily, at ease with each other, no signs of a protest. A block ahead, a long line waited outside a door to the Sorbonne. Maybe it was over, he thought. But when they got to the front of the Pantheon, he saw three police wagons with their engines running and a street blocked off by metal barriers, policemen with submachine guns posted at the intersection. They wore blue jackets with the word "Police" in large letters across the backs.

"What happened to gendarme?" he asked Ariel.

"Globalization."

He laughed, too loud he realized, but pleased that his daughter had made a joke.

Taylor walked on, led the way, paying no attention to street signs, just turning when he saw a building that interested him. He tried to think of comments he could make to his daughter, but nothing seemed right. Finally, he asked her, "How are your shoes?"

"Fine. My shoes are fine." She spoke sharply, as if his question had been an insult.

It was dark now, a faint glow of moonlight emerging whenever the cloud cover thinned. Street lights and shop windows illuminated their path. Taylor found he had taken them to a broad avenue, Boulevard Saint Michel he discovered from a sign, though he wouldn't have recognized it so empty of people and traffic. To their right, on the other side of a green, he saw the imposing shape of a large building wall, a row of pointed parapets at the roof line, totally dark inside. He paused to check his map but found no indication of what it was. Ariel wouldn't know, of course, and he didn't want to admit his ignorance.

"I'm hungry," she said in a tone that implied he should have known.

"Good idea." Taylor realized he was hungry too, but he didn't see any place that served food, walking toward bright lights two blocks ahead, relieved that a brasserie faced the jets of a large fountain across the boulevard. Inside, only one customer, a young man in a grey overcoat, hunched over the bar.

"Is this all right?"

"Yes, yes. Any place. I want to sit."

He pulled back the door for Ariel and picked a table against the far wall covered with a mirror. His chair faced it. "Carte. Menu, sil vous plait," Taylor asked the bartender, a dark round man with a bald head and a moustache. Behind the bar, a boy of about twelve watched closely as the man handed them laminated cards. The boy was shaped like the man, had the same face. Father and son. Ariel wanted a glass of red wine. Taylor chose a beer, a Stella.

When his drinks came and he ordered an omelet, Ariel a sandwich, he lifted his glass in a toast. "Here's to our days in Paris."

She took a sip of her wine and nodded.

After a few silent minutes, he blurted the topic he had been pondering since the plane ride, forgetting the lines he had rehearsed in his head, and just said, "Would you like to talk about your mother?"

"Why would I want to do that?"

"You've been through a terrible ordeal with her."

"Do you really care? You didn't know her any more."

"I did once. Nobody should have to face a death like that. Nobody should have to witness it."

"She was my mother."

Taylor groped for a way to change the subject.

The door from the street opened, and in the mirror he saw the bartender and his son look up from their newspaper, the young man bolt off his stool and hurry to a young woman the moment she stepped inside, enfolding her in an embrace, the wide sleeves of his overcoat wrapped around her back. Holding her close, he guided her to a table, and the bartender followed with his glass.

When they were seated, the young man leaned forward and gripped both her hands in his, his mouth close to her ear, whispering something. Taylor could see that the man was very handsome, a classic French face under dark curls. The young woman had her back to the mirror, her hair dark too, falling to her shoulders. The man touched it with his fingertips, and Taylor thought that it looked very soft, could almost feel the texture in his imagination.

The young man sat back and signaled the bartender, but it was the boy who brought the menus, his father following with a glass of red wine for the young woman. Taylor could see her profile in the mirror as she clutched the man's wrist on the tabletop. She was lovely, as beautiful as the man was handsome. But her expression was distressed, her eyes welled with tears. Something had upset her, and the young man was trying to comfort, reaching to stroke her cheek.

Taylor saw that Ariel was watching them too, directly, not a reflection. The couple's pose reminded him of a scene from an old French film, black and white, the two of them as good looking as movie stars portraying a scene of grief and tenderness, the aftermath of something very sad. Triste.

He leaned over his own table and whispered to Ariel, "What do you think is wrong?"

She gave him a startled look.

"With the girl. Why is she so unhappy?"

"How would I know?"

"It can't be love. She has him, and he's obviously wild about her. Maybe it's grades. She did poorly on a test. Or didn't get a job she wanted."

The bartender's son brought their food, nervous for the plates in his hands, setting them down carefully. Ariel took a bite and chewed, so many times Taylor thought she would never swallow. Then she said, "Her parents. She's had a terrible argument with her parents."

Taylor wanted to say, who could argue with a girl like that, but instead asked, "Over what?"

Ariel shrugged. "They're jealous that she's so pretty."

"That would make them despicable people." Then it struck Taylor: The young woman was pregnant. She had just come from the doctor. Her parents would disown her. Her life had become a disaster.

The bartender put a plate of spaghetti in front of the young man. He twirled several strands on his fork and lifted it to the mouth of the young woman. Her food came a moment later, but Taylor couldn't watch any more, ashamed that he had seen so much. Why should people like that be unhappy, he wondered, aware that was the last thing he could say to Ariel. Father and daughter ate silently. When she said she didn't want another wine or dessert, he signaled for the check. They pushed back their chairs, his making a loud scraping noise. With a last glance, he saw the young man kiss the woman, just a brush of his lips on hers.

He was being foolish. No one suffered for getting pregnant these days. The young woman's woes were a mystery he would never solve.

"I know what it is," Ariel said, speaking low, barely moving her lips.

"What?"

"Someone died. Someone she loves died."

Out on the sidewalk, Taylor realized that he didn't know how to get back to the hotel, which way to turn. He was disoriented. Jet lag. Even the one beer. He could sense that Ariel was impatient, so he picked left, looking behind him at the dark looming shape of the building across the boulevard. Nothing looked familiar. But it was night, and he couldn't see clearly, the headlights of cars dazzling his vision.

After several blocks, they came to a wide avenue with trees along the sidewalk and an island in the middle, a long row of cars jammed at the intersection. Taylor waited for the traffic light, ready to cross to the other side, when he realized the street was blocked off by police wagons, policemen with weapons in their hands gesturing that drivers couldn't get through.

"Do you know where we are?" Ariel asked.

"I'm afraid not."

"Please find out. I'm exhausted."

Taylor stepped under a street lamp to unfold his map and saw that they were on Boulevard de Port Royal and would have to maneuver through a tangle of streets to get to Rue Monge. "We'll have to backtrack, I'm afraid." He turned left and then at the next corner left again into a narrow row of shuttered shops and offices, no lights on the upper levels.

But midway a little old lady with a red hat emerged from shadows. Taylor noticed something in her gloved hand, realized it was a leash, a small round black and white dog waddling at her feet in the gutter. Ariel immediately knelt beside the animal, murmuring soft sounds, stroking the dog's head. The depth of her need made Taylor catch his breath. He had to look away.

He forced himself to speak to the old woman. "Bon chien," he said, and the woman knew immediately that he was not French. "Dix-neuf," she told him, pointing at the animal, holding up all ten fingers and again with just nine. "That's amazing," he spoke in English. "Fantastique." The woman nodded and moved on with her dog.

"Can you believe that?" Taylor said to Ariel. "Nineteen and still going for walks."

She was still kneeling. "The poor thing is desperate to live."

They walked silently for several more blocks, Taylor stopping several times to consult his map. Where Rue Saint Jacques crossed Rue Guy Lussac, Ariel suddenly stopped and sat on a bench. "I can't go on much longer."

He looked up and down for a taxi, knowing it was a wasted hope. He hadn't seen a taxi since they left Boulevard de Port Royal, and only a few there, locked in the traffic. "Why don't you rest for a while?

Taylor felt turned around, unsure what to do next. When he spread his map, he couldn't focus, couldn't locate the street. He had taken them too far, too soon. He had gotten them lost.

The street was quiet, no people out and only occasional cars passing by. Taylor took deep breaths, his back aching, his calf muscles knotted. It was stopping that did it. Standing still. He would be in pain all the way to the hotel. Once he found a way.

Then he heard sirens in the distance, the sound getting louder, and moments later a group of large young men running up the middle of the street toward them, five or six, two tripping over the jutting cobblestones and coming down hard on their hands and knees. They cursed and got up immediately, running again. Not far behind, three policemen were rushing after them, and approaching rapidly, a vehicle with a flashing blue light and a blaring noise.

As the men came close, Ariel stood from the bench and screamed. Don't, Taylor, thought; don't draw their attention. But she was screaming and trembling, and he clutched her just as her legs gave way. She fell against him, so heavy for a woman so thin, dead weight. He squeezed her tight, murmuring, "It will be all right. It will be all right. They don't care about us." They don't even see us, he thought; we're not part of this place.

One of the policemen stopped and lifted his weapon, but when the vehicle sped past him, let it fall to his side. Then they were all on the next block, the young men scattering into alleys and doorways, more policemen scrambling from the back of the vehicle.

Ariel stopped screaming, just stood and sobbed, still wrapped in her father's arms. Taylor couldn't remember the last time he had held her like this, so close to the pulse of her life. "They're gone now. It's OK." He wished he could tell her he loved her, could make himself say the words. He touched her hair and found it stiff, fixed with a spray.

Soon, he knew, she would stop and wipe her eyes, pull away from him as if nothing had happened. He would look at his map and, this time, trace a route. They would walk the final blocks back to the hotel, say goodnight and lie in their beds unable to sleep, waiting for the morning when they would begin their itinerary. For the next few days they would gaze at great art, eat fine food, marvel at the sweep of buildings that lined the Seine. They would stay far from protests and police and rioters and speak of nothing but beauty for the rest of their time in Paris.

Anne Britting Oleson
WE'LL ALWAYS HAVE PARIS

I'm sorting through the postcards in a stall on the Left Bank, across the street and down a bit from Shakespeare and Co. where Jill left me. I feel the eyes of the proprietor, a wizened man in a green corduroy jacket, upon me, but I do not look up. I do not want his sympathy. His little black button eyes will drop anyway if I glance over, back down to the cigarette he's rolling in his nicotine-stained fingers.

I draw out cards randomly, try to imagine myself into the photographs. I'm drawn to people more than buildings. Women. Beautiful women. French icons. Here's a silvered print of Coco Chanel in a suit, the jacket done up to her elegant chin with big square buttons, a pillbox with a wisp of netting perched on her head. She's holding an onyx cigarette holder between two gloved fingers, and I think *that can't be right*. Did Chanel smoke? But everyone did back then. Her head is tilted, her eyes narrowed, and she seems to be mocking me with that steady gaze. I would lean in to light her cigarette, and she would still mock me. *She knows.* I stuff the postcard back into its place.

The proprietor is leaning against his stool, one hand cradling the opposite elbow. He's lit his cigarette now, and takes a slow draw before tipping his head back and blowing a long stream up toward the plane trees, and beyond them the gloomy mid-morning clouds. His glance once again flickers toward me and away. I turn the rickety postcard carousel carefully, select another card. This woman, too, is black and white, a head-to-toe pose; she has flowing drapery pinned with an enormous brooch over one bare shoulder, the rippling fabric both hiding and revealing the curves of breast, hip, thigh. Catherine Deneuve. I stare at the sculpted cheekbones, made more prominent by the cruel bun, pulling the fair hair away from her face. She could be posing for a portrait of Marianne, the French national emblem. I imagine myself the artist, adjusting the pose

— but she waves me imperiously away when I draw too close.

I have to pretend indifference. I slot the postcard meticulously in with the others, run my finger down the entire column before turning the rack again. I don't want to look at pictures of architecture — the monumental buildings rise all around me, behind me, across the river — there's enough here already. It's beautiful women I want. *It's a beautiful woman I want.* Another postcard finds its way into my hand, and I'm gazing now on Brigitte Bardot, her hair free and flowing around her well-shaped head. She sits in a gilded chair, one arm draped casually over its back; she's wearing a tea-gown of some sort, the silky material straining over her breasts, her long legs crossed below the *pouf* of her skirt. She could be taking a breather from whirling with me around the floor at a tea-dance; here she looks relaxed, regal, glad to be away from my left-footedness.

The old man is next to me now, looking down at Brigitte Bardot in my hands. *Magnifique*, he says, tapping the card with the fingers holding the cigarette. He is so close I can smell him, the mix of smoke, of age, of cabbage. He is my penance. I want a beautiful woman, and I get him. I don't move away. I nod in agreement. *Magnifique*, he says again, his voice nearly lost against the hum of the traffic.

When I lift my head, I see the sudden shaft of sunlight fall from the brooding clouds, touching down on the Pont au Double. It picks out a single pedestrian from the crowd, a beautiful woman with an all-too familiar carriage, though she is too far away for me to make out her face. I see her scrub a hand across her cheek, and then, with the brilliant spotlight of the sun on her, she turns and walks away from me, toward Notre Dame, her long blonde hair swirling about her shoulders like a nimbus. Like a halo. Then she is gone.

My sour companion has followed my gaze. Now he turns back and hands me his cigarette. *Magnifique,* he says a third time, but he is no longer looking at Brigitte Bardot. When I glance down at her face, all I can see is a swirl of gold.

Scott Lambridis
RUE BENOIT BUNICO: NIGHT

Every night, around four in the morning, on the rue Benoit Bunico, there is a shouting match between a man and a woman and though they are not always the same man and woman the shouting match always ends with a gunshot. The man is the one clapping and laughing and his voice is much stronger, but the woman shouts more and it is the shrill pitch of her voice that first invades the minds of the two foreigners, a husband and wife, sleeping four stories above the street. "I hate this place," says the wife, turning over in bed, cramming toilet paper into her ears, the rest of her hot and naked, barely covered by the thin sheet. Her husband turns over too, adjusts the paper in his own ears. "Don't hate the place; hate the people," he says. He wonders if he locked the door. Of course he did, the door is a thick slab of metal and there are not one or two but six deadbolts that all lock together when he turns the key. There is no doubt they are locked away inside. The shouting match continues down on the street, in French, which neither husband nor wife understand until, this particular night, the shouting woman's French breaks into the Queen's English — not for long, but long enough for her to say, "Pascal, if you go now, that's it, fine, brilliant, that's just brilliant," and then like all these shouting matches it proceeds again in French and the foreigners pushing the crumpled toilet paper deeper into their ears understand nothing of the shouting. And it does not end until the gunshot sounds.

Julien Green
PARIS: Excerpt

— Translated by Edward Gauvin

I have often dreamt of writing about Paris a book like a long aimless stroll that would lead to nothing you were looking for, but many things you weren't. This might even be the only way I feel capable of tackling a subject I find as discouraging as it is tempting. And first of all, it seems to me I would not say a word about the great monuments and all the places one might expect from a by-the-book description. Perhaps from having gazed too long upon them, I no longer see the architectural glories of Paris with the necessary freedom of mind. Forewarned about each of them, whether for or against, I took sides; I am biased. A thousand times have I wished the Eiffel Tower sunk to the ocean floor; I would be pleased to learn both Palais, Grand and Petit, which deface the Cours-la-Reine, had vanished in the night. My preferences run toward the old stones — I make no secret of it — but I would weep from boredom had I to write a page about the Hôtel des Invalides, because loving it as I do, I wouldn't really know what to say. In the same way, I would remain mute before Notre-Dame, no doubt kept from speaking for shame over what I would hear myself saying, and I admire without envy the bravery of those whom genius or self-importance launches at the siege of such a monster. As for me, I prefer to remain silent, and Notre-Dame remains for me quite simply Notre-Dame, full stop.

•

In my eyes, Paris will remain the setting for a novel that no one will ever write. How many times have I returned from long wanders through old streets, my heart heavy with everything inexpressible I've seen? An illusion? I think not. Often it so happens I will come to a sudden stop before a tall casement window draped in false lace, hidden away in some old neighborhood, and stand there dreaming endlessly of unknown destinies unfolding behind its dark panes. My eyes make out a little bouquet that changes or disappears with the seasons, set in the center of a table covered in dark cloth — and that is all, but perhaps it is enough. Who lives, who dies within these walls? For a novelist, all life, be it ever so simple, retains its irritant mystery, and the sum of all the secrets a city holds has something that sometimes spurs him on and sometimes overwhelms him. What an enormous waste of situations, words, dramatic reversals, characters, mise-en-scènes! How to remain unmoved by such competition? Copying it isn't an option. Only the twits and incompetents copy. No, the only answer is to do something just as good, if possible, with the means at our disposal. And so begins the strange torment of the blank page, in which a window must be opened that is not the one I saw earlier, but of a truth just as pressing and imperious.

•

During the long war years when I lived far away from Paris, I often wondered how the little box of a human brain could contain such a great city. Paris had become for me a kind of inner world in which I wandered in the difficult wee morning hours, when despair prowls about the sleeper who wakes; but it took time before I deliberately crossed the threshold of the secret city I carried inside, for first there were dark weeks in which the mere name of Paris crushed the heart of whoever heard it. And so I closed the gates of the city to myself, I cut off the avenues from as far back as I could. But at night, disobeying my own orders, like a spy or a thief, I would slip down the streets, endlessly making the rounds from house to house. All of a sudden, I would appear in a room where friends were hiding. "Why, it's you lot! And you!" Then a neverending conversation would begin, lasting till dawn. What we could not tell each other, from one side of the Atlantic to the other, we could tell each other heart to heart in these hallucinated meetings. All that water no longer lay between us, I had abolished space, I was there. Endlessly I wished to know. As I was leaving, I would brush the stones of houses and the trunks of trees with my hand, and upon waking, I would have the strange feeling of being at once fulfilled and frustrated.

●

By dreaming about the capital so much, I reconstructed it inside me, and replaced its physical presence with something else, almost supernatural; I'm not sure what name to give it. A map of Paris tacked to the wall would hold my gaze at length and instruct me almost without my knowing. I discovered that Paris was shaped like a human brain.

●

The memory came back to me of a man's head split in two which I had seen, as a child, in an optician's storefront, and which displayed for curious folk the entire inside of the skull. With an interest mingled with horror, I examined that white, pink, and red mass that gave me bad dreams the next night. In vain, told myself it was but an object of cardboard or porcelain; in spite of this, it was appalling. To be fair, it must be admitted that phrenologists, from a delicacy toward sensitive souls like my own, had lent the man with the cleft skull an expression of amiable and almost amused indifference; he didn't mind at all that his entire brain was open to the air and he even suffered with good grace the little labels affixed to every last twist and turn, for therein lay all the interest of this discovery: you were frightened, but became learned; you could see, for example, the seat of memory, or invention, or languages, or reasoning. It was horrifying, but you were excited despite it all at the idea of having, under your hair, two pounds of thinking brain capable of so many things. As for me, I felt at once proud and a bit ill. Today, the phrenologists' man would no longer send the slightest shiver running down my neck, but I am not done marveling over everything our brains can accomplish with a little effort; all it takes is opening a newspaper to see what we've made of the world and recognize, in all impartiality, that we are truly superior beings.

At any rate, more than once the map of Paris helped me through some difficult times, and having found, as I said, that it looked like the human brain, I endeavored to put within that city's limits all the twists and turns I'd once examined. And so it would please me to believe I'd been born in the seat of the imagination and grown up amidst memories; I would dither over where to put willpower, reflection, and taste, ever shifting them from quarter to quarter; sometimes it seemed natural that the capital would recollect its history aided by the Marais, that it perform its intellectual operations with the help of the 5th arrondissement, and its arithmetic calculation in the neighborhood of the Bourse; but crossing through all this was the Seine, which in my eyes stood for everything instinctive and unexpressed we bear within, like a great tide of vague inspirations blindly seeking a sea in which to lose itself…

•

I was heedless, and did not anticipate that with time, this transposed Paris might grow a bit more abstract with each passing day. No doubt I saw it, I always had my eye on it, but sometimes I would get the muddled suspicion that the stones of my city were becoming lighter, as if they had mysteriously emptied themselves, and I was losing, ever so slightly, the sensation of their hardness. How difficult things are to put into words! It was a Paris of visions I now walked in, a Paris that was intensely real, but migrating imperceptibly from flesh to spirit.

•

Right from the first hours of my return to France, I was given to understand just how close matter sometimes is to the invisible through which we move. An ancient desire, almost that of a child, came back to me one day — to climb to the top of Paris to see it as broadly as possible. How many times, in America, had I begrudged myself for never having gone up the dome of Sacré-Coeur? That was where I wound up, led by a shameful provincial curiosity, mixed with an impulse of old tenderness. I made the murderous ascent, reached the sky, closed my eyes with a great lurch of innards, and then, forcing my eyelids open, I looked. It seemed that I took the entire city into my breast. That was how it was given back to me. Winter was drawing to a close; already the blinding light of March was devouring everything, and as far as the eye could see, there was Paris, wearing like a coat ever slipping from its shoulders the shadows of great clouds the wind chased from one corner of the sky to the other.

•

This enormous mass of stone — I had seen it too many times for it to surprise me. And yet, how well it kept it secrets, with what dark violence it existed! Black, sown with tiny flecks of sunlight that mimicked the waves on an unsettled sea, the city was not beautiful, it was immense, it exceeded all efforts of the imagination to depict the kingdoms of the world gathered at our feet, and in its immoderation, there was an excess that provoked anxiety, like a challenge to unwritten but formidable laws.

It was clearly the city that attracts anger, the city perpetually in danger because, faced with temptation on every possible scale, it has never known how to tender the great refusal that might have sheltered it from its own fate. Its domes and towers give an indefinable impression of standing up to someone, and there is something determined, glorious, and undefeated in the very way they are set about this stormy plain. Indeed, the city smiles only on those who approach it and wander its streets; to them it speaks a familiar and comforting tongue, but the soul of Paris reveals itself only from afar and on high: in the silence of the sky is heard the great and poignant cry of pride and faith that the city raises toward the clouds.

Gladys Swan
THE TURKISH MARCH

From the apartment upstairs came the notes of a new piano piece. A relief at first. For Peter had listened to the last exercise repeated so often and with so little improvement he came to hear the wrong notes even before they were struck. Not that it much mattered. The tune, slight and sentimental, jarred him less in the execution than in the sheer repetition. Mercifully, the teacher had sent her pupil on toward a new, if uncertain destination. Peter thought of either a small, possibly humpbacked creature with pale skin and pink scalp showing through thin blonde hair, or else of a graying invalid. For him, the source of error seemed located in physical deformity. Who would be playing at this hour of the afternoon but one cut off from the world of work or school, at the time of day when he himself took a rest and tried to gather strength for his evening round of shopping?

But now he listened. Having established the melody with one hand — a melody immediately familiar, which maddened him for hours afterward without his being able to identify it — the player picked herself up and went on, introducing a new motif. Expectation strained forward as the notes came one after the other, slow, hesitant — wrong. A new start. But no better. She (invariably he thought of the player as she) kept going back to the beginning, determined, it appeared, not to play the whole until she could play it right. Till finally she gave it up, for that afternoon. But the melody assailed Peter from the heights of something perfectly mastered and immediately meaningful to the emotions — quite beyond reach. He sighed and got up, too restless to sleep. For the remainder of the afternoon he took to his newspapers and was lost in the political stupidities from across the Atlantic. Even at this distance, they set his teeth on edge.

•

That evening as he returned with his demi-baguette and strawberries, his cauliflower and lettuce, his breakfast croissant, he had his first exchange with the woman who lived in the apartment overhead. He held the door open for her, a small woman with a powerful inner determination that seemed to press her beyond the burden of her packages and her terrible bridgework. His sympathy went to her the moment she smiled. Who had done such a botched-up job? A front tooth at that, yellow, oversized, mismatched with the good tooth it was anchored to. Metal underneath. He wanted to punch the dentist in the mouth, yank out a few teeth for his pains. The woman was afraid to smile. The bastard hadn't given her a chance.

They climbed the stairs, avoiding cigarette butts and wrappers and other trash on the steps. Earlier in the afternoon they'd have had to work past the motley crowd waiting for their turn at the bell of the second floor apartment: mostly young, dark, nervous, except for a large well-groomed fat man, and a svelte black woman who looked disdainfully upon the scene around her. *La Clef d'Or,* a sign announced. *Sonnez et entrez.* Buyers of gold. Where daughters could sell off their mothers' necklaces and thieves could fence their loot. A jittery lot, Peter noticed. Keeping one eye out for the gendarmes, chain-smoking, crushing the butts on the steps. The smell of smoke hung in the passage, mingling with the evening's bourgignon.

"A terrible mess," his neighbor said in French. Despite her various parcels, she carried herself with dignity, moving almost as slowly as he did. She frowned, drawing in her nostrils, and looked at him. Her eyes, the soft and luminous irises set in a dark ring, had a complexity of expression that drew him: knowing, skeptical, yet eager, sympathetic. Above the ruined smile.

"As if the hallways weren't dirty enough," she continued. "I've complained to the concierge, but she merely shrugs. Sometimes I kick the butts down from one step to another — right to the bottom. Let her see them there." A flash of defiance from the eyes.

Two dogs inside La Clef d'Or barked as they passed.

"Tch. And the noise," she said. "It's bad enough on the streets. You can't escape."

He agreed to all of it, still upset by the yellow tooth. What had possessed her to go to such an incompetent? Lack of money? Ignorance? You never knew what you were walking into. Trusting and helpless you went, and somebody took your money and did a number on you. The clown probably soaked her plenty. "Where can you go these days... ?" he ventured, breathless from the climb. Who had turned the monster loose in the dental profession? What mentor had passed him on, signed his certificate, inflicted him on the public? He should have gone into politics — there, who noticed?

"They had the cops here last month," she continued, this time, to his surprise, in English, perhaps thinking he had more difficulty with the language than with the stairs. She gave a little smile when she saw his expression — nicer when her teeth didn't show — then took up her indignation. "Someone tried to break in, the burglar alarm went off, the dogs went berserk, the whole building in an uproar. Sirens. Gendarmes. Everybody on the stairs, in the courtyard. A big drama, I tell you. I thought of moving out, but what's the good?"

"The world's gone mad," he said. "Hijackers, terrorists...." He could have created a whole list if he'd had the breath, but he still had one more *étage* to go. At least he'd had the good sense to move in after the commotion. Otherwise his blood would have been up, and this time he might have enjoyed the services of a foreign hospital. But what did it matter? He had come to Paris to die. It was as good a place as any.

"I shudder when I go by," his neighbor complained, nodding in the direction of the Clef d'Or. "The way they look at you. Like they've come from slitting somebody's throat."

"Probably their mothers'," he suggested. They had arrived at his floor. "Do you play the piano?" he asked suddenly. Clearly she hadn't expected such a question. But then she gave a little smile, melancholy and tender, "No, my granddaughter. I hope it's not disturbing you. I could..."

"No, no," he protested. "I love music."

Having unlocked the three locks on his door and put the door between himself and the street, he began to wash the lettuce for his salad.

He didn't know her name; he'd forgotten to ask. He liked her face, the fine eyes. He was still troubled by the ruined smile.

●

He discovered that on certain days they went to the shops at the same hour. Once they'd passed each other in the market, but his neighbor was so preoccupied she failed to notice him, and he didn't want to startle her. Some evenings he didn't see her at all. She must work then, but not always at the same hours. And her granddaughter must be home alone all day. He was curious about her. His neighbor must prepare her meals ahead of time. He could hear her saying, "Now for lunch, there's a nice bit of sausage, and you can heat up some soup." All he knew was that after lunch the child (young woman?) practiced the piano.

"So you're an American," his neighbor said, when they met again, this time after they had introduced themselves. Sophie Mitkin. Peter Sziv.

"I thought so, though your accent isn't typical. I was in the States for six years. My teenage years," she said, with a rush of pleasure. "I love the States."

"Actually," he said, I was born near Budapest, though I grew up in South Bend." Which she probably never heard of before. In a whole community of honkies, like one big family, eating, drinking, dancing together, marrying one another, going to the funerals of friends and relations. His mother and father working their lives down to the bone marrow. Citizens. The great achievement. They could claim his bloody carcass too.

"My people are Russian," Sophie told him. "My parents came from the same village, though they didn't meet until they were grown and here in Paris."

A young Chinaman, squatting illegally in the empty maid's room on the sixth *étage*, passed them with a bundle of laundry, greeting them shyly.

"When were you in the States?" he asked.

"During the War," she said significantly.

One of the fortunate refugees. The pure race — it took a dentist's mentality to think that one up. Add it to four thousand years of the might of the stronger, and the displaced person. Humanity by the teeth. They had reached his landing. "By the way," he asked, "do you know the name of the piece your granddaughter's practicing?" He avoided the word *playing*.

"Of course," she said, her eyes brightening. "'The Turkish March.' Mozart. Did you see *Wuthering Heights*? Merle Oberon. Lawrence Olivier. They go to a ball and a woman plays it on the piano. A wonderful film. I saw it six times. I remember every scene, and I could always see myself…" She stopped, embarrassed.

Going to the ball like the wild Katherine. He completed the fantasy for her. Charming. He wished his own had been as harmless, even as they had been bootless. Friend, he'd thought, of revolution, assistant to change. Holding cupped hands for the flare of the match, as he played spy for Army Intelligence. Two or three days high on amphetamines, courtesy of his superiors, forty or more hours without sleep while he and Arno, companion in folly, combed the Hungarian countryside, mingled in the towns to gather news of the direction and prospects of that doomed and betrayed revolution. Then back to their base in Austria to drink a bottle of bourbon and plunge into oblivion until they were sent out again. Only youth and a strong constitution could withstand such punishment — for a time. After the tanks came, he was put to the task of resettling refugees, in charge of the whole effort in Yugoslavia. He had written various papers for the U.N. Years later, back in Chicago, he still kept in touch with some of those he'd sent to the States. The grateful owner of a delicatessen, who heaped upon him gifts of his favorite sausage, a musician now battling leukemia, a lawyer for those with claims in Hungary. And Arno was there, grown prosperous in the import business, married to a fashion model, the two of them traveling back and forth to the Europe he could never quite leave behind.

The habits of his old life had made drinking a necessity, a nightly pathway to oblivion. Most nights it was a wonder he got home at all. Once he'd awakened in an alley. Even while Arno was warning him and his own wife nagging at him in the hangdog way that made him want to kick her, he knew it was coming. His liver, his heart — what didn't turn against him? Fortunately he'd kept all his army records. From the government he received compensation for total disability. Money at least, was no problem. When he was on his feet again, so to speak, he told Arno to find him a place in Paris.

•

She'd never been a beautiful woman, Peter decided, not even when she was young. Though her smile still disturbed him, it was becoming part of how he expected her to look. In the company of the prominent nose, the splendid eyes. Probably she'd never been slender either. Always a little extra in the arms and breasts, extra padding on the hips. The cheekbones, the eyes you couldn't see to the depths of, the full mouth, they had gotten her a husband, maybe a lover or two. Imagining herself at the ball. Imagining passion. The extreme you pushed everything toward. In America, her Russian sensuousness. At her high school they must have looked at her, stood back, wondering whether or not to touch. He tried inventing a past for her, seized on what he took as their common bond: the various dislocations that had brought them to apartments just above one another. To which they both climbed the stairs slowly.

He closed his eyes, tried to disengage his mind from the struggling performance overhead and sleep. He could have shut the window, but he needed air. He had chosen the middle of the afternoon, while the shops were closed, to rest, to rescue his strength so that he could go out to buy the makings of his evening meal. Though the fruit and vegetable stands were mobbed then, the *boulangerie* where he bought his half loaf of French bread, and standing in line tired him, still he liked the press of people in the streets. It was his social life. His anonymity allowed him the privilege of being merely a spectator upon the scene: housewives, French, oriental, African — all sorts; clerks and businessmen en route home, jostling elbows, winding through the press of people. Finally, all of it was less than nothing to him.

He was alone. No one left except a brother in Toledo he hadn't seen in years and had no desire to see now. No claims on him. His health was shot, his useful life was over. And the uses of that life were now so distasteful to him he woke up at times trembling and sweating, the sheets twisted around him. He could seldom remember the details of those dreams, but they soured his mood for hours afterward.

●

"My daughter brought her to me," Sophie said, "and told me, 'Please keep Marguerite' while I go on vacation. She wanted to go to Los Angeles, where there was something going on. She was divorced then. 'French men are so boring,' she said. 'There are no jobs. I need to find myself.'" He and Sophie were sitting in the café just opposite their street. Sophie was eating liver pâté. He was having a salad. Red meat and cheese were bad for him, so he lived on chicken and fruit, bread and salad. He liked the discipline of his diet, though this time he allowed himself a glass of wine.

"What could I say?" She shrugged and offered her open palms. "What is there to say to such discontent? I said to her, 'Go and explore then. There is always such energy in America. You'll find a place for yourself and Marguerite.' I kept waiting. One postcard, then nothing. I tried writing her hotel."

"You contacted the embassy?"

"No. I didn't want to cause trouble for her. I didn't know … Even now, I say, surely she'll write."

"When was this?"

"Three years ago." Sophie played with the breadcrumbs on the tablecloth. "She had no patience with Marguerite. She's an unusual child. She can't stand butter on her bread — it gags her. She used to scream if she saw chicken cut up. She won't eat any meat. Whenever Paulette went to buy clothes, she would hide under the dress rack. And school— impossible. She would soil herself so they'd send her home. Poor thing, and she hates so to be dirty. It's too much for her. She drove the teacher wild. I can't tell you how many days I had to take off from work to go to the school. So I took her out. I have a student from the Sorbonne who comes once a week to tutor her. She likes to read, especially books with pictures."

"She doesn't get lonely?"

Sophie shook her head. "She watches a little television, plays with her cat. Sometimes she likes to go with me to the Tuilleries. She holds my hand in the métro. Occasionally we go to the museums. She likes the cinema. The Indonesian girl who cleans —— they're great friends. Then of course her music…"

"How old is she?"

"Nearly twelve," Sophie said, "but she looks like eight."

"What will happen to her?" she said, putting down her fork, pressing her napkin to her lips.

He poured more wine into her glass, but she did not touch it. She twisted the corner of her napkin, looked off into space. Then she recovered herself, smiled, lifted the glass and held it to the light, as though proposing a toast. Ruby red, dark, with a gleam at the center. "We're the only ones left," she said.

•

What would happen to her? he asked as he listened to her play —— this violation in the logic of generation. For the world, she was an idiot, not of intelligence but sensibility. And Sophie and he were two of a kind. Time was nearly finished with them, ready to throw their carcasses aside. Time for him meant waiting. The color of time had changed, now that illusion, expectation had dropped out of it. Slowness on the stairs; pill bottles on the shelf. The neighborhood with a restless surge of blacks, East Indians, Orientals, coming from who-knows-where, living who-knows-how. Bombs on the Champs Elysees, in Le Magasin. Time was a dark rush that would soon enough drop him too.

Now she could play the "Turkish March" all the way through, and there were passages that kept the proper notes and rhythm. It was clear that she liked the piece, for certain phrases leapt past the notes toward a suggestion of triumph. But she had no control. The piece came patched with repetitions, new starts, uncertain passages. For him, it became those errors and repetitions. He lay in bed every afternoon listening for something that might be called progress, but error dogged her. Hopeless. He could never sleep. It wasn't her playing that kept him awake, but his own disquieted mind, going round and round with the latest absurdity in the Middle East or Latin America, the most recent piece of corruption he'd read about. For every day he read the newspapers, French and American, with the avidity of an addict, the fascination of a man watching an anthill.

Like folds in a sheet of paper, the lines of history crossed and intersected his, Sophie's lives, turning things awry, creating the inescapable before and after. He often thought of this when they were together.

The two of them met now on Fridays for their dinner together, the night she worked late. By then Marguerite would have eaten, watched television a little, and gone to bed. She did not practice in the evenings for the sake of the neighbors who might want quiet then. The fat man on the other side felt no such constraint, but practiced his trumpet with impunity, even sometimes early on Sunday morning.

"Before we left for the States," Sophie was telling him, "there was a wonderful year. My father was rich then; we lived in a beautiful house and I had lovely dresses. But even then I knew. One day a fine house, the next day, broke and on the streets. My father was like that."

She had accepted casual elegance like the weather. Expensive restaurants, good wine at the table. A governess.

"He had a radio station then in North Africa. The Germans wanted it, but he wouldn't sell. Of course they wanted to kill him. We had to leave everything with only a few hours' warning. I remember he spent the night burning papers." Other things she would not speak of.

In one of his recurring dreams, people kept moving, running, falling into shadows in unknown territory. His life had been given to this ambiguity, this struggle.

"I loved it aboard ship. The captain was very kind to me. Always showing me things in his cabin. It was a wonder my father permitted it. He let me blow the boat whistle. Each time he did, two Indians would say, 'It was just like that the last time — they blew the whistle just before we were torpedoed.' The passengers asked me, please would I not blow the whistle." She grew animated as she spoke of her youth.

She had been happy then. When she came back to Europe — but before she could tell him, a police car whipped past, followed by an ambulance.

"My God, it's right here in the neighborhood," she said, standing up. "Look, there's a crowd."

"Our building," Peter said.

She went white. "Marguerite! She's alone. Oh, dear God, I hope nothing's happened."

He leapt up to pay for their dinner

She was trembling. "I just want to satisfy myself she's all right."

When they arrived at the apartment, bystanders filled the sidewalk. The ambulance was in the driveway that led to the courtyard, and someone was being carried down on a stretcher. The concierge was talking to the gendarmes. "Who is it?" Sophie asked around her.

"Robbery. The Clef d'Or."

"They shot the woman. In the head."

"Is she dead?"

"Imagine — with all the dogs barking."

"They knew the place. They did something to the dogs."

"Her husband was away."

"Is she dead?"

No one seemed to know. The ambulance shrieked off down the street, and they were allowed to enter the building. Sophie hurried up the stairs.

•

Marguerite is ill, he read on a note that Sophie left under his door. I am staying home to take care of her.

For a number of days no sound came from the piano. He telephoned once to ask how she was. Sophie had come up the stairs to find Marguerite hysterical. The shots ringing out, the sirens. The first robbery had left her terrified. This time she developed a fever. She didn't know where she was.

Where could you step, he thought, but into the fevers of the mind? From the flower seller be bought daisies (marguerites), and some bonbons and asked the concierge to take them up. He'd seen the child only once, from the back. Hair dark like Sophie's. Small for her age. He wondered if she had Sophie's eyes. She must be a pale child, from being deprived so much of the sunlight. Would Sophie take her to the park down the avenue when she was better?

He'd come across a crippled veteran there at the entrance on his way back from the post office the other day. He was wearing a ragged overcoat and held out a can for coins, at the same time ranting and waving his cane. Whether denouncing the government or swearing at those who passed by indifferently, Peter was unable to tell. He was unshaven, possibly drunk. They have saved a place for you on all the métro cars, he thought; one has to stand and give you a seat. On the other side of the park, a Vietnamese woman with a baby held out her hand. "For the baby," she said.

When he saw Sophie on the stairs, the flesh of her jaws looked heavy and her eyes were tired.

"How is Marguerite?"

"Better, thank you. Tomorrow I'll go back to work. The concierge will look in. I'm going out for strawberries," she explained. "They're her favorites." She smiled. "I used to pick them when I was young — in the country they grow wild."

He was relieved. The mother would never return. Sophie must know that as well. What sort of life included Marguerite? Better to unzip the past and step out. Poof — it's gone. She'd gotten a face-lift maybe and gone on the most recent crash diet and exercise program, bought a new wardrobe and had a lover who thought her accent adorable.

He was entertaining these possibilities when he heard again the first notes of "The Turkish March." Shaky. She was badly out of practice. And she'd never play it well. Not like the woman in *Wuthering Heights*. Not anything close to what Mozart had in mind. But she was back at it.

He would see Sophie again. He would sit across from her and listen to her story of how she'd come back to Europe after the war and found every aspect changed, how she'd wept over leaving her friends behind, her other life. She didn't know a soul in Paris. The flat was so cold she spent hours in bed reading, far into the night after the rest of the household was asleep. It was her only real pleasure.

"The Turkish March." And who remembers the Armenians? The jumble of history knocked in his head. Marguerite had gone back to the beginning. And he was again prepared to hear another version of that much-patched piece. Gradually she took hold of the melody. He wondered if she'd like to go for a picnic in some quiet place, the Bois du Boulogne or somewhere farther out in the country. Perhaps Sophie could take a day off during the week when there would be fewer people. He would buy strawberries and search for a bakery that made the good tough French bread now so difficult to find.

He drifted deeper, the melody enticing him like a conjuration, her playing of it fused now with that intimation of form that danced beyond the notes, calling up somehow the taste of strawberries, the image of Sophie's eyes, luminous and dark, her yellow tooth and jagged smile. Separate, yet blending as a single sensation; for a moment, all contained. His chest rose and fell in rhythmic breathing. He let go and fell asleep.

Essais

Andrei Konchalovsky
JULIETTE

— Translated by Bryon MacWilliams

Various things can be demanded from an actor. There is some kind of balance between that which can be expected, creatively, and that which can be imposed by a director. In movies an actor can be placed under severe stress, demanded to produce, because the action isn't continuous — merely a concentrated fragment, one shot from beginning to end. In theater, though, there is no beginning or end, but a continual flow of life. On the stage an actor needs to live. And, for that, a director must create a world for the actor — a world of people who love each other.

For the revival of Chekhov's play, *The Seagull*, at the Odéon-Théâtre de l'Europe in Paris, we brought together such people from all across France. We needed to select actors who not only loved each other, but felt a spiritual oneness with the characters, the personalities, on stage.

I scheduled auditions. A good number of people showed up. Toughest of all was finding the person to play Nina Zarechnaya, the daughter of a rich landowner.

The movie star, Isabelle Huppert, came. But she didn't want to try out.

"I'm interested in the part," she said.

"You'll need to audition," I said. "Read."

"Why?" she said. "I'll still wind up with the part, I think."

The wonderful actress Barbara Sukowa traveled from Germany to audition. She had been in movies by Margarethe von Trotta and Rainer Werner Fassbinder.

A young woman showed up, too — Juliette Binoche. She had just finished shooting in the American film by Philip Kaufman, *The Unbearable Lightness of Being*, which was based on the novel of the same name by Milan Kundera. She also had been in a film by Leos Carax.

Binoche had a porcelain face with downy white skin, and cherry lips. She was small, fragile, very flexible. Later, in bed, she would remind me of a marmoset bounding about... But I'm getting ahead of myself.

"Read," I told her.

She began to read the monologue. Not bad. Still, I was unsure.

"Will you come and read again?"

"I will."

"Then come."

Again she came. She read the monologue. Again, not bad. But I wasn't yet convinced.

"Will you come again?" I asked.

"I will."

She came again. She read, again. Some other young actresses showed up, too, but, still, we kept looking.

Binoche returned yet again. Again, she read.

"Will you come again?" I asked.

"I will."

She read for me five times, and she was prepared to read even more. I felt uncomfortable inviting her back, yet her persistence intrigued me.

Then I received a letter from her, in the form of a poem, in which I was depicted as a cross between a lion and a tiger. The poem was quite beautiful. It was in French, too; I didn't understand half of it. It ended with this line: "I want to play the part."

The letter even included a drawing to that end. It was a lovely letter.

I invited her to coffee. We fell into conversation. By profession she was an artist; her father was a sculptor.

I invited her to a performance by Roman Polanski in Kafka's *Metamorphosis*. Sitting next to her in the box I had only one desire — to caress her neck.

So that's what I did. She didn't remove my hand.

She belonged to another man, lived with him — Carax, the cult director of French cinema, the director who had made her career. I knew that she was being courted, too, by Daniel Day-Lewis, opposite whom she played in *The Unbearable Lightness of Being*.

Day-Lewis had fallen in love with her, apparently. I didn't rule out that they had been lovers.

I remember once riding in an elevator with her, when I literally felt a pain run through me — the kind of physical ache that happens when one is in love. Apparently I made a face because Juliette looked at me and asked, "What's wrong?"

I skirted the subject. And I didn't kiss her, even though I desperately wanted to.

When I think of love and nonlove, the only true criterion for me is pain. Love is pain. Everything else is nonlove: falling in love, having a good time, or loving feelings toward a woman, a father, a mother, a brother, a friend, God.

Painful means sweet. One can even weep from the sweetness of pain.

Love, too, is a loss of control over oneself. And I don't enjoy losing control over myself. I hate it. You fall in love, you no longer belong to yourself. Still, the older I got, the more reckless I became.

That moment in the elevator signaled a long, typically Russian process of seduction that bordered on sexual harassment. Russian men are like that, clinging to a woman like a wet birch leaf clings to the skin in the banya, the Russian bath. (I'm this way, even though my astrological sign is Leo.) We don't have any sense of distance or pride, unlike Germans or Brits. They're proper: if a woman let's you know she's not interested, it usually ends there.

I continued to try to wrangle out of her some kind of reciprocity, but, with the exception of that night at the theater, she continued to try to avoid contact. I don't quite remember how it all unfolded, but one day we were sitting in a café, playing a game: beneath the table I held her knees closed, and she tried to open them.

My head swam. I fell in love.

Juliette wound up with the part of Nina, and we began rehearsals in a suburb of Paris. She unvaryingly stayed till the end each day; for her, there was always something more to do, and she tormented everyone. (Later, she would request a teacher of movement, and worked with him daily, prior to rehearsals.)

After that we shared our first kiss, in the theater. The first kiss, particularly when you really love a woman, isn't simply a touching of lips. Above all it is a gauging of her reaction. Women react differently to a kiss. One blushes, becomes shy, while another turns away, shudders — or slaps you in the face. Still, that reaction is a sign, a symbol of desire (or lack of desire) for physical closeness. That desire to be penetrated can be felt even when a kiss, on the surface, appears innocent.

I told her one day at rehearsal that I'd meet her in the theater at such and such row, in such and such box.

"Right now?" she asked.

"No," I said. "During the break."

She nodded her head.

It was all I could do to wait for the next break. We each took off in different directions, then met on the third level, in the second box. It was there we kissed. It was effectively our first date.

From the box we could see the theater, the stage, everyone with whom we were working.

We did this every day: We met, we kissed, then we returned to the hall from different sides of the stage — me with red ears, her with rosy cheeks.

I used my official position to my personal advantage, as they say. Fine, so be it. It didn't disrupt rehearsals. In fact, it only helped them. I felt a rush of inspiration, enthusiasm.

A theater. Balconies of red felt. I had the sense that everything was unfolding in the time of Molière.

Eventually we took a liking to a box that was closer to the stage; the break was only ten minutes, after all, and it took time to get to the third level, then get back.

I evinced the pure form of Trigorin, the novelist in *The Seagull*. I even have a photograph of myself seated among the cast, wearing the costume of Trigorin. And she was Nina.

Only, unlike the play, it was me who was in love. Head over heels.

Once, when we met in that box — ah, that red theater box! — we hugged, fell to the floor, and rolled across the dusty red felt.

She whispered: "You... It's you... Finally... You're the man of my life."

She spoke the words so passionately! Rarely — never, perhaps — have I been told anything quite like it. Her words struck me like a blow to the head. For the rest of rehearsal I felt as if I were walking around, intoxicated.

Alyosha Artemev, who had come to write the music for the production, was a witness to our romance. The three of us often went to a Vietnamese restaurant where we drank sake. I wanted the role of Nina to be played as if she were a porcelain figurine — only very malleable.

Indeed, Juliette is much like a sculpture. And with her arduous work ethic, and powerful memory, I was able to draw out of her movement that bordered on choreography. For the role she had to fall, clown-like, while doing a cartwheel, then somersault back up. She performed it brilliantly.

Juliette lacked, perhaps, an element of tragedy. But, in every other respect, she was spectacular. (Actresses who perform Nina Mikhailovna Zarechnaya do well either in the first three acts, or the fourth. For an actress to perform well across all four acts is exceptional, very nearly impossible. Juliette was that exception.)

Across the street from the theater was a bistro. Once, after rehearsal, Artemev and I were sitting there when she showed up. We all drank a little, then she looked at the clock and said, "Well, it's time for me to go!"

Carax was waiting for her around the corner. With their dog.

She left the cafe and soon could be seen, with him, on the other side of the street. She looked somewhat sad, if not despondent. Her appearance gave me a modicum of hope.

After the performances were under way, Carax became jealous. She left him, told him she couldn't live with him any longer. She took all her books.

We decided to spend the night together. I was mute with feelings of both elation, and horror.

"My God!" I thought. "Could I really be so lucky?!"

She took me to her apartment. I was afraid to merely lie next to her in bed, and out of fear blabbered some kind of nonsense. Men can be afraid to sleep with women they love, but she didn't suffer from such a dilemma. French women, in general, possess a Cartesian approach to sex. I'm not saying that they can have sex and, at the same time, read the newspaper, or talk on the phone. But they bring a certain lightness to sex — don't spend time trying to make it elegant. Afterward, they can seemingly forget about what just happened and run off somewhere. But I only realized that later...

Juliette, of course, is a French woman through and through. She has an easy way with men — in the best sense of the word.

My happiness that day was very brief. We arrived at her apartment after midnight, around 12:30. At around 1:30 the phone rang. She began to get dressed.

"Who is it?" I asked.

"Leo."

"Huh?"

"He wants to see me. He's in a bad way."

She finished dressing, grabbed some things and left — just like that! I lied there, confused, in her bed.

Our relationship nevertheless continued on, and it was painful — a triangle of bohemian, artistic love not unlike Truffaut's film, *Jules and Jim*. She also had had an affair with Day-Lewis, yet, each time, she kept going back to Carax.

After it was over I felt as if she, in fact, had been cheating on me — that her declaration that I was the man of her life had had no basis in fact.

Usually, after performances, I would drop by her dressing room and we'd drink tea, and talk. One night I went to her dressing room and knocked, said, "It's Andrei."

No answer.

It struck me as strange. Could she have dressed that quickly?

I waited about 15 minutes, then stepped away from the door — but not before overhearing light whispers and muffled giggling.

I understood that she simply didn't want to see me. Her dalliance with me was over. I was alone, again, and at peace in my soul.

Debra Marquart
THE PERILS OF TRAVEL

Should we have stayed
at home and thought of here?

— Elizabeth Bishop, "Questions of Travel"

Something that unnerves me when I fly on certain European airlines is the way that passengers will applaud at touchdown, as if a crash landing were the norm, so an uneventful landing is a cause for celebration.

On most U.S. domestic flights I've taken, safe touchdown is so thoroughly assumed that passengers are out of their seats, threading their arms through coat sleeves and eyeing the overhead compartments even as the plane's back tires screech down. The cabin crew urges over the intercom, "Please stay in your seats! The captain has not turned off the fasten seat belts sign."

But on several European flights I've taken, conversation hushes at descent. Greeks, Russians sit up straight, look forward, spread their hands flat on their armrests. Are they thinking of loved ones or concentrating on keeping the plane in the air, as I am? Once we hear the concussion of the back tires on the tarmac, the cabin comes alive with applause. Passengers turn to each other and smile. They nod their heads at each other as if to say, "That was good, no? Again, we did not crash."

Perhaps I've imagined all this. Perhaps international flights are just traumatic for me, an American, because they remind me of how much farther away from home I'm taking myself, which forces the natural question — if I die abroad who will repatriate my body? Will it be my new boyfriend, my ex-husband, my mother, or some odd combination of all three working together? I imagine them collaborating, making travel plans on the phone after they've called each other to deliver the news of my demise. But how will they even find each other without my address book?

Will my ex-husband and my boyfriend travel together to pick up my body, my mother being too old and fearful of new places to go herself, and my new boyfriend being too new and too aggrieved to travel by himself? I imagine them sitting together on the flight — my new boyfriend and my ex-husband — two gorgeous dark-haired, dark-eyed men accepting their hot hand towels, their complimentary glasses of champagne, flirting, perhaps, with the flight attendant. How dare they! And on the way to pick up my body. It makes me want to live, just to deprive them of the experience.

Americans are rather like bad Bulgarian wine: they don't travel well.
— Bernard Falk

Some travelers, I have observed, take the earliest opportunity to imperil themselves when they arrive at their destinations. The bag is barely unpacked before they must climb the highest bell tower or ride the shaky tram suspended by frayed cables to the peak of the nearest mountain. They must take the creaking elevator to the top of the Eiffel Tower, or huff up the three hundred odd steps, cobbled together in the 16th century, we are assured, by the finest of Europe's masons, to the lean tip of the ancient cathedral. They must stand in the crumbling eye of the wind-blown spire and, if that's not enough, step out onto the shaky platform with no guard-rails. I've never had such a desire when traveling.

On my first trip to Paris, I unwittingly enlisted myself in a perilous adventure with Scott, a fellow American I met at my hotel, the Grand Hotel Des Balcons. I suppose it was the sadness I observed in him each morning as he ate his 50 franc breakfast, cracking his hard-boiled egg, spooning his yogurt so thoughtfully, and reading a book in English, I noticed, which first made me aware that he was likely an American.

When I saw him days later, walking along the rue Casimir-Delavigne with that same English novel tucked under the sleeve of his brown corduroy jacket, I felt compelled to stop him and introduce myself. We talked like old friends on that windy street, just off the busy St-Germain-des-Pres, and discovered that we were both writers — he, from the West coast; me, from the Midwest.

In minutes, we disclosed a great deal about ourselves, as travelers and Americans tend to do, and especially as traveling Americans do. I liked him immediately and found it a relief to speak to someone in fluent English after ten days by myself in Paris during which time I had communicated mostly with hand gestures — exaggerated facial movements, and confusing English fragments, which I delivered in what I thought to be a French accent. I don't know why I began speaking broken English with a French accent as soon as I arrived in Paris. But it only seemed that my English was better understood when I did so.

Talking with Scott on the sidewalk outside our hotel, it seemed exhilarating to be gushing English to someone and to have someone gushing English back to me. I liked him, but I wasn't attracted to him. Not in that way you imagine you might someday be attracted to someone you meet when you're traveling and unsupervised, in that no-one's-watching-anyway, one-night-stand kind of way. His hair seemed too neatly combed, I think, his clothes too uniform. Plus, there was this business of his overwhelming sadness.

Even though he smiled a great deal as he told me that he was treating himself to this trip to Paris as a reward for completing his first novel, he did not seem to be a man who was celebrating. Soon I discovered the reason — he was newly divorced, had a young daughter whom he missed terribly, and, to add insult to injury, his newly-divorced wife was a quite famous novelist. I pretended to be impressed when he told me her name, but really it only made me feel more sad for him.

He told me that the next day would be his final day in Paris, and that he had planned to visit the Catacombs buried under the city of Paris, then finish off the day with dinner at The Procope, an upscale restaurant in Paris that bore the distinction — or at least claimed to bear the distinction — of being the oldest eating establishment in all of Europe.

As if on impulse, Scott asked me if I'd like to spend the next day with him, and just as impulsively, I said yes.

There is no greater bore than a travel bore. We do not in the least want to hear what he has seen in Hong Kong.
— Vita Sackville-West

The next morning after breakfast, Scott and I set out in good walking shoes with our water bottles and backpacks. As we climbed above ground from the Denfert-Rochereau Metro stop, we walked a bit before coming upon the entrance to the Catacombs on the edge of the 14th arrondissement.

I had traveled to Paris to find some traces of my immigrant family's original culture. Even though my family had emigrated from France to Russia in the early 1800s, and then to America in the early 1900s, I still felt, as I walked the streets of Paris, an affinity — the food, the smells, a gesture, the curve of a cheekbone, the angle of an eye. I saw my brother, my father, my sisters each day as I walked down the streets. Given that between five to six million people had been buried in the Catacombs over the course of the last two centuries, I thought it would be as close to visiting a family grave as I would get while visiting France.

Scott and I waited in the long queue forming outside the entrance. At eleven AM, the doors flung open and the line began to move. To my right as we filed quickly through the lobby, I noticed a map mounted on the wall showing the cavern we were to enter — 1.5 miles of underground walkways full of bones. The Reliquary tunnels, I had read in the guidebooks, were created in the 12th and 13th century out of the giant caverns that resulted from quarrying the limestone that was used for buildings, churches, ramparts and monuments all around the city of Paris.

The first burials in the Catacombs were necessitated by health concerns during massive plague outbreaks in the 1780s. The numerous skeletons were dismantled, reorganized by part, and interred below in neat piles of skulls, femurs, fibulas, and tibias. Death, the great leveler. As one guidebook announced, no distinction for class or political persuasion was made here, "the skull of a revolutionary may be resting on the leg of an aristocrat; noble and corrupt, young and old, wealthy and poor, all are indistinguishable now."

As we waited in line, I had some horror-movie-imaginings of what we would find below — shelves of laughing jaw bones, long bony-fingered hands, heaping piles of yellow, clacking teeth. The guidebook said the Reliquary was dark and the crypt floor was covered with lime.

The book advised to wear good shoes and bring a flashlight. Always the careful traveler, I had packed two flashlights and a compass.

At the Catacomb entrance, Scott and I were pulled by the momentum of the crowd through an area cordoned off with red velvet ropes. We threw our 35 francs each at the woman behind the plate glass window and dashed to the right where a man in a red suit pointed to a slim descending staircase straight ahead.

Down we went, following those ahead of us. The stairs were narrow, just room enough for one person, and they curved downward in tight 360 degree revolutions. I took one complete circle down the staircase, then another. The people in front of me tramped ahead briskly; I matched their pace. The people behind us pushed and moved as we moved. We were descending deeper, making one revolution down then another when my feet began to go numb.

My lungs grew heavy in my chest. I halted in mid-step and grasped the handrail. The people ahead of me on the staircase rushed headlong, disappearing down and down the spiral into the cavern. An emptiness opened beneath me on the staircase. I could feel Scott's weight behind me and all the weight of anxious tourists that accumulated up the steps behind him — everyone mad to get underground and see the famous cache of bones.

"There's no one coming up." I whispered, as if I'd uncovered a government conspiracy — France's solution to the problem of too many American tourists?

"Scott," I said, "this staircase only goes one way."

"What?" Scott asked. His voice was strained and breathless.

"I can't go another step." I sobbed.

"Oh my god," Scott said with alarm. "Are you claustrophobic?"

"I don't think so," I said. Then I realized I, really, sort of, was. I don't like elevators or crowded rooms or basements without windows. Now I recalled the passing glimpse I'd taken of the Catacomb map on the wall. The red dotted line marking the underground walking path — 1.5 miles — that would finally deliver you to the exit. I realized this was all a one-way trip.

"Oh my god," Scott repeated, realizing the situation. "One time I was in the middle of the Golden Gate Bridge, and my feet stopped moving just like this."

He was saying this to comfort me, but the image of being stranded in the middle of the Golden Gate Bridge didn't help. In fact, it made me begin to hyperventilate, since I'm even more afraid of water and heights than I am of small spaces.

I should have known better than to attempt the Catacombs, but they were a common tourist attraction, all the guidebooks said so. Every year thousands of families — teenagers, infants, toddlers, parents — rolled down this staircase in their khaki shorts and Planet Hollywood t-shirts to take a gander at the acres of dismembered skeletons. This cavern has been in use for over seven hundred years — revolutionaries, bandits, peasants, workers going in and out at all times of the day and night.

It takes supreme arrogance, I realize, to believe that the day *you* choose to visit the Catacombs, the eight hundred-year-old cavern will decide to give way and bury you and all the unfortunate other people who descended with you on that day. It goes along with being Catholic, I think, the belief that the very particular finger of God is always on just-you.

I'm also certain the centuries-old smoldering volcano will blow the very day I visit; I know the hook-echo of the tornado is heading for my front door. I wouldn't risk the observation decks of either the space needle or the leaning tower of Pisa, nor would I linger around the Acropolis too long, lest the ancient ruins decided to become completely ruined on the day that I visit.

Now that I was frozen on the Catacombs staircase, there was no arguing with my body. I tossed the flashlights and compass in Scott's direction and grabbed the banister. "Go on without me." I threw my shoulder like a wedge into the dozens of tourists pressed behind him, and I began to scale the stairs.

"But where will you be?" Scott asked as I moved past him.

"I'll find you," I shouted back, "wherever you exit." It sounded dramatic, even as I said it, like when Daniel Day Lewis yelled to Madeleine Stowe in *The Last of the Mohicans* as she was being abducted by unfriendly Apaches, "Stay alive, no matter how long it takes, I will find you."

Scott grew smaller and smaller as I climbed higher. "Tell me everything you see," I yelled, pulling myself up like a salmon swimming against the current. The going was slow.

People muttered in every imaginable language as I squeezed past them. I apologized my way up the curving handrail, ex-cus-e-moi-ing and pardon-me-ing as I climbed. When I reached the ground level opening, the people waiting to descend parted for me to climb out. Without a word, the man in the red suit opened a velvet rope that led to a side exit. He didn't look surprised; I suspected this happened more than a few times a day.

I circled around to the front and swam through the crowd to have one quick look at the map in the lobby which listed a street level exit point several blocks away called the Ossiary Exit. The word, *ossiary,* with its close association to ossifying and ossification made me shiver. I had a palpable moment of claustrophobia even then, just imagining myself gasping for breath, trapped in that underground cavern as it collapsed around me. I sprang out of the front door of the Reliquary entrance, driven by the strong impulse to breathe and be supple in my limbs.

Outside, it was a cool, summer morning, not even noon yet. It felt good to breathe in the clear air; the sunlight shining hot on my face. I wandered for blocks in this new light and open space, elated with my good fortune for being this very breathing, above-ground being.

Travel is glamorous, only in retrospect.
— Paul Theroux

I wound up on a grassy berm somewhere near the boulevard du Montparnasse where so many American writers have sat in smoky cafes and discussed great, developing works of art. The lawn felt so green and open-air against my skin that it was hard to believe that tourists were paying money to walk underground and view the ancient bones of by-gone Parisians.

I walked a few more blocks finding only unfamiliar street names. I began to worry. In his backpack, Scott carried the guidebooks and the map back to the hotel. He had navigated us here on the Metro. I had no good idea of where in the city we were.

Ahead of me on the boulevard, I saw three women approaching. I resolved to ask them for help, and I prepared myself for a rebuff. In my experience, men all over Europe will help a single woman. A woman traveling alone seems to be an affront to European men. If you are lost, they will offer to walk you to your destination. If you are eating alone, they will insist you join their group at dinner; they will pour you wine from their carafes, offer cigarettes and matches to light them, then invite you to come along for drinks or a coffee afterwards.

Struggling with my bags in European train stations, I have had men pick up my heaviest suitcase, carry it onto the train for me, and go on their way without a word. The friends to whom I've expressed this observation say cynically that the men were simply trying to pick me up. This may be sometimes true, but I don't believe it is always so.

For the most part, I've observed a civility in Europeans that Americans do not possess. Lost in a large American city, I expect and hope to be left alone, to flounder in my lost and aloneness. In Europe, I know I will be helped. But my observation has also been that European women are less friendly and helpful; just as, in America, I am less likely to help strangers. This is perhaps true all over the world because women must be more mindful of their personal security.

"Pardon me," I said to the three approaching women. They were French, each one more tall, slim, and angular than the next. "Can you tell me where is the Ossiary Exit?" In my broken English with a fake French accent, it sounded like a bizarre question.

"Ah, an American," one of the women said with excitement. She fell on me and grabbed my arm as if I were her sister.

"Yes," I conceded. Usually I tried to conceal my Americanness, even declaring myself a Canadian if times got desperate, and speaking with crisper enunciation and emphasizing my higher, rounder vowels, which I got from growing up in a high, northern state. When I travel, I try to dress well, refusing to wear the typical American tourist costume — tennis shoes, khaki shorts and an untucked t-shirt with a logo from some garish American franchise like the Hard Rock Café. I find the better dressed I am when I travel, the better I am treated by everyone I encounter.

Now I spoke in English to the three French women, who listened attentively. I spilled it all out — about the Catacombs, my panic, my surprise at my claustrophobia. The most friendly woman seemed to have the best English. She held my forearm as I talked. All three "No'd" and "Yes'd" through my story, then they had a short interchange in French. They talked quickly, nodded, and clicked their tongues; they didn't need to translate. *The Catacombs, yes, a ghastly place.*

They were beautiful women, long-limbed and elegant. They walked six blocks out of their way to show me to the Ossiary Exit, then the friendliest one kissed both my cheeks and deposited me on the dusty stoop overlooking the opening.

I sat on the curb after they left, drinking a bottle of mineral water, and watching as countless tourists ascended the steps from the Catacombs. Many of them came through the Ossiary Exit, short of breath and perspiring. They emptied out onto the sidewalk, many of them ashen-faced, bending over, taking deep gulps of air as they stepped into the light.

You could see that the journey through the cavern had been an ordeal for them, as I suspected it would be. But when, I wondered, had it occurred to them that danger was possible or imminent — somewhere deep underground, when it was too late? Either I was too phobia-laden and full of trepidation to be a truly intrepid traveler, or I had an early-warning system programmed into my DNA, the same thing that impelled my ancestors to flee revolutions in France then Russia.

My family line had survived, after all, because my ancestors had known to read the early warning signs and flee the instability of Alsace in 1803. Their descendants had known to pick up stakes and flee the growing instability of Russia one hundred years later. Even as a wild young woman in 1960s America, seemingly racing toward the brink of destruction, I always knew before my friends when to put on the brakes.

Far travel, very far travel, or travail, comes near to the worth
of staying at home.
— Henry David Thoreau

Scott appeared eventually up the Catacomb steps. He was happy and perspiring, but not traumatized in any way from his journey through the Underworld.

True to his word, he told me everything he had seen as we walked back to the Metro stop — the long, dark tunnels, the dripping water, the bone heaps, piles of craniums, the walls of bones quilted with patterns of femurs, and, near the end of the trek, the clear water drinking fountain of Lethe, or *de l'oublie* which invites you to drink and forget all that you have seen on your passage. Showing the greatest restraint and good taste, Scott did not ask me about my panic on the stairs or question me about my claustrophobia.

Later that night, after I bathed and put on a fresh, black dress and sandals, I met him in the hotel lobby and we walked the few blocks in the Latin Quarter to the Procope. The food was good as I recall — oysters on the half shell with mignonnette sauce, brazed duck with glazed shallots, chocolate souffle for dessert — but the waiters glared at us with the delivery of each platter.

In between courses, we licked our wounds by making fun of the scowling waiter, deciding that even though The Procope boasted the longest run of any eating establishment in Europe, they still had not perfected their style. In all the meals I had in Paris, before or since, it was the only one in which I was treated badly.

Scott insisted on paying for the meal, the price of which I knew was exorbitant. We walked back to the hotel in silence. It was his last night in Paris. We collected our keys at the hotel desk under the suspicious eye of the clerk, and walked together up the spiral staircase of the Hotel des Balcons.

I recall inviting him into my room, because it seemed rude not to do so, even though I didn't have any wine or coffee or cognac and chocolates to offer him. He sat on the edge of my bed for a time and we talked about writing. He talked about his early flight, calculating how much time he should allow for getting to the airport in the morning. And then he left, perhaps seeing that I was not interested in anything more than talk.

At the doorway, we double-kissed each others' cheeks and exchanged business cards. We promised to e-mail, but we never did. In the years since, I've looked for his published novel, putting his name into the search engine of Amazon from time to time. As far as I can tell, his novel has never appeared, although his ex-wife, I have observed, continues to get more and more famous with each passing year.

Thomas E. Kennedy
YOU DON'T REMEMBER ME, BUT I REMEMBER YOU

For Janet McDonald (1954-2007)

This is about a girl I met a few times and knew for a few years, and with whom I shared a fondness for soul. She was so kind, before she died, to make a tape cassette for me that she titled, "You Don't Remember Me, But I Remember You" which she also referred to as "the world's greatest music."

Her name was Janet McDonald, and she grew up in the Projects in Brooklyn, one of seven children in a small apartment, and went through some hard times with junk and guns and crime before she graduated, a scholarship student, from Vassar with a B.A. in French literature, from Columbia with a master's in journalism, and from N.Y.U. with a degree in law. Then she relocated to France as a lawyer for an international law firm where she seemed to have found some measure of happiness before she died, far too young. Her problems with junk and crime, contrary to what one might assume, were not from her years in the Projects; they only started when she was at Vassar and N.Y.U., only then did she find herself getting raped, tasting heroin, packing a pistol in her belt and firing from the roof of her dormitory building up into the sky.

But in Paris, as far as I could see, she was happy.

Then she wrote an autobiography — *Project Girl* (Farrar, Strauss & Giroux, 1999) — about her difficulties and triumphs, and the international law firm in Paris that she worked for acknowledged her achievement — getting the book published by a major New York house and winning praise from Frank McCourt, Rosie O'Donnell and many others — by firing her. She went on to write several books of young adult fiction for FSG.

I met her in Copenhagen, where I live. I grew up in lower middle-class Queens and couldn't get away to Europe fast enough. Life in America was no better for me than for her, for different reasons that one day in the last year of the last century intersected. She phoned me and said she had my number from a mutual acquaintance who had told her that if she was ever in Copenhagen she should make sure to call me. The mutual acquaintance was one whose name did not ring a bell with me, and I asked where Janet knew her from; she told me that she didn't know her at all, met her in passing at a party in Paris and happened to mention she was about to go to Copenhagen, and the person in question urged her to call me. We shared a laugh on the phone at the prospect of our being introduced in Europe — a girl from Brooklyn, a boy from Queens —by a mutual acquaintance neither of us could recall! I liked the sound of Janet's voice and of her laughter so we agreed to meet by the bank on the corner of the North Gate Station, a place that many people pick as a meeting spot in Copenhagen.

Unfortunately, I forgot to ask what she looked like or to tell her what I looked like or what I would be wearing. Standing in front of the corner Danske Bank, I kept glancing expectantly at various women — young, old, short, tall, slender, plump, blond, brunette, gray — until someone touched my shoulder (maybe she had checked my picture on the web) and I turned to see a woman about ten years younger than I —then in my mid-fifties —slender, dark close-cropped hair, a slim triangular face, big smile and black complexion. I remembered Andre Dubus writing about how he and Kurt Vonnegut, Jr., were to meet Ralph Ellison at the Iowa City train station and had a long discussion about what they would answer if he asked them how they had recognized him instantly. But that was the early '60s; this was the late '90s —just nine years before Obama. I searched her eyes for amusement at what no doubt appeared as surprise in my own eyes — I just hadn't guessed that she was black, and the slight surprise I felt taught me something about myself. Not that I didn't know any African-Americans — a third of the guys with whom I'd been in the army were black; and that had been my first experience of black people and it was a very positive one.

Janet did not look like your typical international attorney — she was wearing jeans and a dungaree jacket. I don't remember where we went, only that we had agreed to meet for a beer, which is different than agreeing to meet for a coffee — meeting for a beer involves a certain amount of risk, trust, daring — and that we had a few and that I felt a bit of pride sitting with a fine-looking black woman ten years younger than me in this ancient north European capital (that's how shallow I am). I also remember that somehow we got to talking about music and that we both loved soul.

After she got back to Paris she put together a tape cassette for me which she titled, "You Don't Remember Me, But I Remember You." Two of the numbers on it were songs that I had told her had a special place in my heart, one of which — "Hello, Stranger," by Barbara Lewis — I remembered being saved by, one desolate night in 1963 in the fly-infested, stinking-hot, August-humid barracks in Fort Benjamin Harrison, Indianapolis, when I was in the Army — it saved me by making me remember a great day I'd had at the beach with a girl I was crazy about and who let me kiss her. I had been unable to find that song on a record since then, and Janet hunted it down for me. The second was a song that my very first girlfriend had played on the radio in a call-in dedication for me, "Tears on My Pillow" by Little Anthony & the Imperials in 1958. I was touched — not simply because Janet had done a kind thing for me, but also because — and this might sound odd — we clearly were not romantically attracted to one another — or I guess it is more accurate to say that she somehow made me understand that she was not romantically interested in me so I kept my hands to myself — but we *liked* each other and because of the extreme unlikelihood that we would ever have met were it not for the person whom neither of us knew who had put us together. There was so much against us having run into one another: our color, our oil-and-vinegar New York City boroughs, our class, the country we were living in now, our schools — hers Ivy League, mine whatever the opposite of that is …

I read her memoir with enthusiasm and interviewed her for *The Literary Review,* and we exchanged a few emails. I remember once writing to her, and her responding something like that she had thought I had decided I hated her because it had been so long since she heard from me.

Which startled me. I really liked her. I suppose she was joking — but as the Danes say, he who understands a joke only as a joke and sincerity only as sincerity has equally misunderstood the two. We exchanged a few more e-mails, met once or twice in Paris for dinner — I recall one restaurant we dined at in the Sixteenth, across the Seine from the Eiffel Tower, around the corner from the apartment in which Marlon Brando and Marie Schneider explored one another's psyches in *Last Tango* — for lunch, for a gathering of expatriates on the Contrescarpe. I read some of her writing, she read some of mine, but we lost contact. Somehow, after seven or eight years, we fell out of touch.

Then, in 2010, visiting Paris to give a reading at Shakespeare & Co., I met a mutual acquaintance — Ellen Hinsey, the American poet — and Janet's name came up. "Whatever happened to her?" I asked. "She stopped anwering my emails." Ellen looked at me with concern. "I thought you knew," she said. "Janet died three years ago." She had had cancer and died in April 2007, just fifty-three years old.

When I got back to Copenhagen from that visit to Paris, I searched through the shoebox in back of my closet in which I had pitched my old tape cassettes (this being the post-casette, about-to-be post-CD age) and was relieved to find the one she had made for me over a decade before. Rubber-banded around it was the play-list she had emailed me with small comments beside some of the songs:

"'Time Is On My Side,' Irma Thomas (those thieving Rolling Stones!)";

"'Piece of my heart,' Erma Franklin (Aretha's Sister!)";

"'Piece of My Heart,' Janis Joplin (put in for contrast; she whips Erma's butt!)";

"'Go Now,' Bessie Banks (those thieving — I forgot their name!)";

"'The Wind,' The Jesters" [I had told Janet about this original version of that song from 1959] and "'The Wind,' Laura Nyro and LaBelle (featuring Patti) — I only knew this version)" — and the only version Janet had known, recorded thirty or forty years after the Jesters' version is one I had never heard before, although I was wild for Laura Nyro — also dead much too young.

She had concluded her play-list by writing, "So there you have it. I'm off to work. Janet."

Now I climbed up the narrow back staircase of my building to my attic storage room to see if my cassette player was still there. It was. Back in the living room, I slipped in the tape, and listened. I loved every number on it — our taste for soul really had jibed; they were definitely among the favorites of my lifetime, the background music of the women I had loved and lost or never had in the first place. And it occurred to me how important this music was and is — and how it united Janet and me across all the gaps that had separated us — class, color, borough, school, country — and now across the gap that separates life from death. Sooner or later — probably sooner given my fairly advanced age — I will be dead, too, and it seems, unless all the after-life fairy tales are true — unlikely that Janet and I will meet in any after-life so we will never again have the opportunity to see if our body moves and rhythms could have conjoined in a dance to one of these songs. Maybe "Hello, Stranger." Oh, how pretty it would be!

But equally remarkable was that several of the numbers on the tape touched memories in me of girls I *had* danced with — despite the fact that I cannot dance, there had been in fact a few — precious few — times in my life when I had managed to dance with a girl as naturally and pleasurably and sweetly as pie. To people accustomed to dancing, this must seem a strange boast — but I have little doubt there are others who share my usual two-left-footedness from which I am only very, very rarely reprieved. Ah! But then...

I listened through to the end of the tape, reversed it, filled an ice bucket, broke out my best vodka — black label Stoli — and played the tape again, savoring each number, remembering those dances, those girls, some of the highlights of my life, complete with background music — remembering Janet.

I can still see her face — smiling — when she surprised me on that corner in Copenhagen during the last year of the last century.

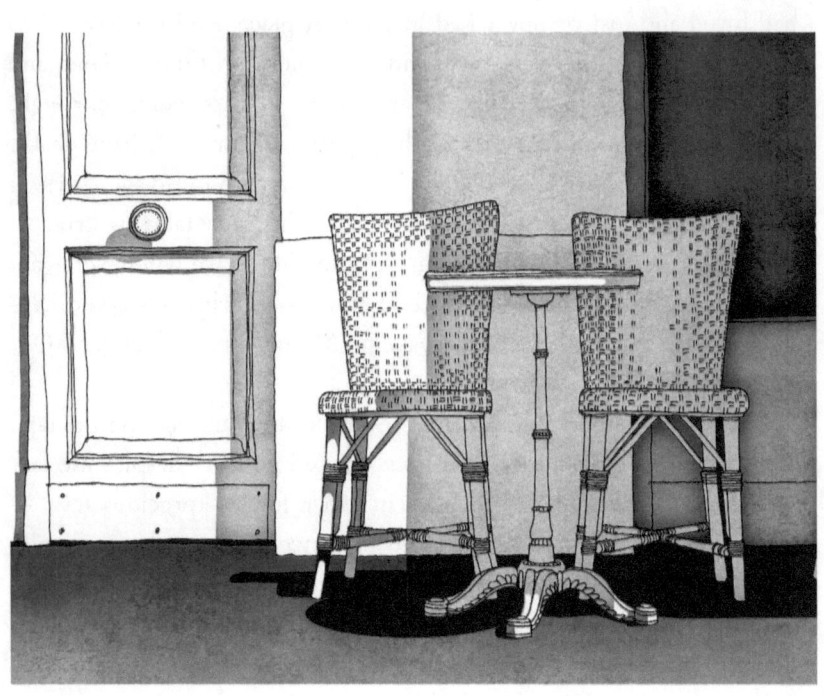

Bettina Ballard
THE REBIRTH OF PARIS

On a July morning in 1945, after my return to Paris, I awoke to the cracking pistol-shot noise of metal shutters being opened, to find myself in my own wide, comfortable bed in which I had listened to the declaration of war six years before. The same maid, Marcelle, bought my breakfast, her hair by now grown out enough from the shaving it had been subjected to after the liberation to be frizzed into its habitual tight curls. The coffee she brought me was good leftover PX coffee, the rolls fresh. I was a civilian again, my time and my house were my own, and I was very happy. I had rescued my bed only the day before from the attic of the son of the great baritone, Jean de Reszke, where Cousin Isobel had hidden it from the German officer and his mistress who had lived in my flat, and when I had sunk into its deep, wool-stuffed comfort, a flight of moths soared out, irritated at being disturbed from such a large source of food supply.

Around me that July morning were my trunks of clothes and linen that Marcelle had packed carefully and put in storage in 1940. I began poring through them with delight, finding all of my exaggerated prewar hats, which looked even sillier now, my favorite red plaid Molyneux suit, my beautiful Parma-violet velvet Chanel suit, and many pairs of high-heeled evening sandals — sandals that I later sold to the concierge at an outrageous price suggested by her. She wore them from early morning, when she dragged the heavy trash cans across the cobbled courtyard, through the day when she washed my big linen sheets on the stones of the courtyard with her skirts tucked up showing astonishing high silver heels, to the evening when she clattered down the quiet rue Las Cases to the corner bistro to have a drink. The shoes were an indulgence that she permitted herself from the profits of the black-market eggs and butter smuggled in from Normandy by her old taxi-driver father.

Putting on my red plaid Molyneux suit that morning, I was still happily unaware of how little conditioned I was to civilian life. The protecting hand of the military had fed, transported, and entertained me for two and a half years, and my ability to fend for myself was temporarily atrophied. My PX card was gone, my easy entree into any army mess hall was a thing of the past. I could no longer call up a friend in the Air Force and ask for a car or a ride in an airplane — a bicycle was my transportation. I was a civilian outsider now, and any favors were out of order, Even when I went to dine with old military friends it was a little like going back to visit an office for which you no longer work; everyone is glad to see you, but you are slightly in the way of their daily business. I wasn't part of anything at the moment. I was in a sort of terminal-leave-get-back-to-reality stage that had its uncomfortable moments.

There were no restaurants open that summer of 1945 in Paris and rationing was still on. My first walk up the rue de Bourgogne, whose generous shops had supplied me before the war, showed me only a few potatoes or tomatoes on display, procurable with ration tickets. My butcher supplied me with two delicious and fancily molded pats of ground beef for my weekly meat ration. My sister sent me food packages from America with rice, tea, sugar, and soup mixes (Marcelle was shocked at the idea that any good soup could come out of an envelope), and instant coffee. But none of this was enough to take care of my natural inclination to say, "Come and lunch," or "Come and dine," when I ran into friends. I would find myself with guests and nothing to give them. I would take my bicycle, which the concierge had hidden for me during the war, and ride with a sort of frenzy in my heart and in my stomach up the quai to the house where fat Marie (Louie Macy's old cook) now concocted rich dishes for Charlie Wertenbaker, the Paris bureau chief for *Time* magazine, and his pregnant wife, Lael. I would find Marie trying to force a freshly made cheese croissant, dripping in butter, down the nauseated throat of Lael. I would eat half-a-dozen croissants greedily myself, ask Lael how she was feeling, and sneak out to the kitchen on some pretext or other to ask Marie, in a whisper, if she had a gigot or a filet to sell me. Marie wasn't in the black-market business herself but she always believed in having provisions "in case," and I was an old friend. Sometimes my filet would cost me twenty-five dollars with a few potatoes thrown in. Marie had never left Paris during the war, and she had the very best possible relationship with the best possible black marketers. She almost ruined Charlie Wertenbaker financially that summer because all of his friends found Marie's cooking so superlative and it made her so happy to make the American liberators so happy. The only unhappy aspect was the state of Charlie's pocketbook and his expanding girth.

There was one particularly famous dinner early in the summer that Marie herself gave in the Wertenbakers' flat for her old *patrone*, Louie Macy Hopkins and her husband, Harry Hopkins, who were on their way home from a visit to Stalin in Moscow, after the German surrender. This dinner celebrated lots of things: Louie's visit, Lael's pregnancy, the liberation of Paris, old friendships — it had to be as good a dinner as Marie could make it, and no one who went was apt to forget it the rest of the summer. That was the night when someone complained to Louie that she hadn't called her back, and Louie replied, "To ask anyone to call you back in Paris is the best brush-off there is." That was before the P.T.T. rid its offices of the mice that had been happily gnawing the telephone wires in Paris for years, and put in automatic telephones to outwit the uncooperative telephonists. This was the first time that I had seen Louie Hopkins since my disappointing tea with her in Washington when I was joining the Red Cross. I felt ill at ease and childish about it in retrospect but Louie was so obviously unaware that I had ever been upset that we immediately fell back into our old easy relationship.

When I went to dinner with opulent French friends, I was surprised to go through the same prewar menu of soup, fish, meat, salad, cheese, and fruit, as if there was no such thing as rationing. The French had no scruples against using the black market or provisioning themselves from their own or their relatives' country places. It would have seemed absurd to them, and certainly not very *débrouillard*, not to take good care of themselves if they had the means or the influence to do so. There was no stigma at all attached to running a good kitchen or running your car, if you could wangle the food or gasoline.

There was more than my search for food to depress me in Paris. I found everyone in the *Vogue* office in a state of tired lethargy, as if the war and last winter's cold had left their blood in a dormant state. There was no momentum; the office was like a house full of clocks that hadn't been wound. Even Madame Dilé's birdlike gaiety was quieted to that of a sick bird, and Leone, De Brunhoff's lovely doe-eyed secretary, had sad, resigned circles around her eyes, like a captured deer. Everyone in Paris was tired. They had had so much to pit their wits and energy against during the German occupation that, now that there was nothing to oppose, nothing to stimulate their *esprit de contradiction*, they sagged mentally and physically. This spirit gave me little to report to American *Vogue* and left me with no outlet for my energy. I understood their reluctance to face reorganizing their lives and their politics. But I wanted them to yawn, to stretch, to awake and feel the stimulation of activity again. Even my valiant old Cousin Isobel had finally succumbed to the tiredness accumulated in her war years, and she lay in the American Hospital with pneumonia and a bad heart. I bicycled out to see her whenever I could, silent under her oxygen mask, but with her courage to live still functioning.

As unenergetic as people were about getting back to work, socially Paris was still active. The hard core, the nugget of social life that summer was in the British Embassy over which Lulu de Vilmorin ruled while Alfred and Lady Diana Duff Cooper were ambassador and ambassadress. Here was to be found the "little group," the type of inner exclusivity that Paris loved so dearly, the closed set where conversation was in a particular jargon, almost incomprehensible to the outsider. Marie-Louise Bousquet and Minou Montgomery lived near me in the Place du Palais Bourbon. I went to Marie-Louise's Thursday salons, filled now with war correspondents who had discovered her wit, and to the Countess Montgomery's crowded supper parties where I was apt to meet the Glouie of Marrakech, the top French generals (one of whom Minou Montgomery married), and all of the pretty society women of Paris. When the Arturo Lopezes returned from New York after the war, they resumed their dinners in their beautiful house in Neuilly with as much pomp as restrictions allowed.

Drew Parsons that summer was one of the most popular hostesses in Paris, doing much of the wonderful cooking herself. She had been a great friend of Louie Macy's and mine in prewar Paris; she has turned into a resistance heroine during the war and had written a book about her experiences. She had married Geoffrey Parsons, Jr., who was editing the resuscitated Paris *Herald Tribune* brilliantly. They lived in a lovely flat on the Ile St.-Louis overlooking the Seine. It was always worth the long bicycle ride there for dinner as their flat was the meeting place for every amusing or important person going through Paris, with always a sprinkling of French politicians, newspaper editors, and war correspondents, the latter beginning to feel that their free-wheeling exciting life was about over and hating it.

Drew's most endearing characteristics of exaggeration and improvisation were in direct contrast to Geoffrey's factual knowledgeability. I remember his careful respect for facts well as I used to bother him constantly for information for a guidebook to the United States that I was writing that summer. He would never give me an answer unless he was one hundred per cent certain of his facts, when all I wanted was a good fast guess that had some chance of being closer to fact than my guess would be.

The guidebook was not a work of inspiration on my part. A publisher with a name that sounded like a Balkan state, Ogrizek, had made a quick war fortune putting out a lavishly and amusingly illustrated guidebook to France, which he sold to the German occupation forces. He thought he had struck a good thing and wanted to do a similar series on other countries. He offered me a big sum to do the one on the United States, and as I did not have enough *Vogue* work to keep me occupied, I accepted it, farming out many of the states to *Herald Tribune* staff writers. No guidebook has ever been more inaccurate or written from more varying points of view. The only reference books we had were the W. P. A. series that we found at the American library. I can remember writing that the Battle of Bunker Hill was the start of the American Revolution. It didn't really matter because, translated into French by Ogrizek's secretary, who understood little English, it sounded like gobbledegook anyway.

I don't think that the publisher made another fortune on this book, but I did buy quite a few Paris costumes on the proceeds.

Georges Geoffroy, who hadn't a sou when I left Paris, was now very prosperous, with a flat on the rue de Rivoli filled with signed eighteenth-century pieces of furniture — all from the proceeds of finding treasures for his friends and showing them how to decorate their apartments. Georges was a person of importance in Paris, decorating a house for the newly returned Honourable Mrs. Reginald Fellowes, doing rooms over for Arturo Lopez, and introducing Gloria Rubio as a great beauty to Paris. Paris always has to have a current beauty who is the rage. That summer of 1945 it was Gloria Rubio, who was — and still is — a great beauty, dark and slim with an aura of mystery and adventure about her, two beautiful Gainsborough children by her side. She appeared from Spain, elegant in her black-and-white Balenciaga clothes, her long, slim feet shod in Helstern's slimmest last, her diamonds very white and discretely worn. Georges introduced her to me, and I quickly photographed her for *Vogue* as the Princess Fakhry and, later, as Mrs. Loel Guinness. Aside from being beautiful and, as Balenciaga said, the most elegant woman he dressed, she was more fun than anyone else I saw in Paris that summer. When she would revert to being pure Mexican, which she was, she would take down her black hair, which she coiled sleekly on the top of her head, let it fly loose around her shoulders, and dance like a gamine. She never really believed in society, refusing to allow herself to be lionized in Paris, preferring to be with a few people she liked at a time. She took an apartment that summer on the far edge of the Bois de Boulogne where I often bicycled for lunch or dinner. I remember coming home one night in a delicious summer rain, braving the fabled satyrs of the Bois as I pedaled along singing at the top of my voice from the sheer pleasure of the exercise and being wet to the skin — a pleasure that I associated with running through the sprinkler barefoot when I was a child.

The couture collections went on as usual the summer of 1945, as they had gone on all during the war. I can't remember much about them except that Balenciaga was still making his handsome suits with snugly buttoned bodices and rolling peplums. I quickly ordered a black-and-white one with a velvet collar. René Bouché came over from New York to draw the collections with me for American *Vogue* and, more important, to take his wife and son back to New York. They had been caught in Paris during the war when he was a German prisoner. Bouché rented a bicycle at an outrageous price so that he could get around with me — a bicycle much too big for him, which made it difficult for him to jump off and on when the gendarmes held up their white batons for us to stop. With bicycle clips on the trousers of his very city suit and his obvious unfamiliarity with a bicycle, I felt very superior as I rode with one hand and made the proper signals with the other.

The night of V-J we Day we rode our bicycles up to Montmartre, certain that we would find there some sort of celebration over the final end of World War II, having found no sign of enthusiasm or interest around the Opéra or the Champs Élysées. After pedaling up the hill toward the Place Clichy, we found ourselves lonelier and lonelier, with no sign of life other than the Montmartre cats courting from one side of the street to the other. We were walking our bicycles dispiritedly when we heard the shrill voice of a woman echoing down a narrow street from in front of a small hotel. Standing under the single blue light was the usual Montmartre girl in tight skirt and swinging handbag arguing with a slim-hipped American sergeant. *"Deux milles, vous comprenez — un, deux milles,"* and you could visualize her counting on her fingers. Then we heard the voice of the American sergeant. "How much? No *comprenez*." And again the lesson in counting from the woman, *"Un, deux milles, comprenez?"* Finally he comprenez-ed, for he rocked himself back on his heels and said, "Listen, baby, we came over here to save your asses, not to buy them." Then he strode toward us, muttering to himself savagely, "These God-damned Frogs, and on V-J night, too!"

After the collections, Bouché and I went to England to do a story on postwar London. British *Vogue* had arranged for us to stay in a private flat where we were given breakfast by the lady of the house — grilled tomatoes, toast, and strong black tea — as hotels were still occupied by the military or officials of one sort or another. Britain was a great shock to me. After my years with the military, where privileges are taken for granted and where there was always a way of getting what you wanted if you knew the right sergeant or the right general, and after three months in Paris where any Frenchman would consider himself or anyone else stupid not to use every means at his disposal to get what comforts and privileges he could, I wasn't prepared for a country where people frowned on privileges, where rationing was accepted by all classes, where integrity, fair play — all the qualities I had been taught as a child to believe in and had conveniently forgotten — were in full force. I saw the long queue of women in the street waiting patiently for sausage that was mostly meal when they bought it. I felt the cold and damp of the British *Vogue* office that had had no heat for years, and I saw the rough hands of the fashion staff, chapped from cold water, cold raw air, poor nourishment, and bad circulation. I was reminded at every step that this was a land of no privileges.

I had asked British *Vogue* to get me a visitor's card for a session in the House of Commons as I had always found this by far the best show in London. The Sergeant-at-arms from the House of Commons had called *Vogue* to say that they were sorry that they could not receive me as they were sitting in the smaller quarters of the House of Lords (the Parliament buildings having been bombed) and there was a sudden very important meeting and the daily press had to have priority. I went anyway, convinced that some way I could wangle my way in. I presented myself to the Sergeant-at-arms as if I had not received his message. He looked surprised but explained it to me all over again, and I, in turn, pleaded that this was my last day, surely he could find one little corner for me. "Even Mrs. Winston Churchill could not have a card to hear her husband speak today," he expostulated. Suddenly I was ashamed — very ashamed — before this invincible integrity, before a "no" that was a no. My respect for England was rising with every rebuff to my own selfish schemes.

At the *Vogue* office the people were like characters out of a play, each playing their daily role while imagining themselves quite different people inside. Harry Yoxall, the director, with his elegant Proustian manner, his pride as a wine connoisseur, watched every scrap of paper, every paper clip that was used in the office, resisted excess use of electricity for warmth, and made British *Vogue* pay all through the war. Audrey Withers, the editor, poured a semblance of luxury and glamour into the pages of what was considered a luxury magazine while believing staunchly in Clement Attlee and the Labour party. The fashion editor went through the motions of understanding the stark, unimaginative fashions forced upon British clothes manufacturers by restrictions while she imagined herself forever clad in diaphanous negligees trimmed in ostrich feathers. The feature editor was a dedicated intellectual producing page after page of what she imagined the fluffy, cotton-filled heads of the *Vogue* readers were capable of absorbing. It all came under the heading of "Carrying on," which they could do for Condé Nast as well as for England.

On my return to Paris I had a letter from Edna Chase, asking me if I would like to come back to work in New York, hinting at a much more important job. I had already had an inkling of what this job might be when I had been in New York on leave in May. Babs Rawlings (Babs Willaumez had married the young photographer whom she had helped soar to success during the war) had told me in confidence that she was fed up with being fashion editor, that she had never liked organizing other editor's work, and that John Rawlings wanted her to help him with his increasing advertising photos. She was holding on, she told me, until I returned. I had paid little attention then, knowing how Babs had forever been about to leave *Vogue* and never did. But Edna's letter made me think that there might be something definite brewing.

I had given little thought to my postwar life or where I would live it. The summer in Paris had not revived my enthusiasm for living there permanently. I was dismayed constantly by the French cynicism, their inability to believe in the ultimate importance of anything except their own families, their overcivilization. In 1939, when war broke out, I had felt a relief from tension, a hope that after the war everything would be different in Paris. Now everyone seemed intent on reconstructing their lives as nearly as possible to their prewar pattern. I knew that my life in Paris would continue on the superficial lines established by my *Vogue* association. This life didn't impress me any more; it left me with an empty, unsatisfied feeling. The surface luxury that I knew I could have in Paris, the clothes, the false importance of my position, the longer vacations, the traveling, the lighter work, all had to be weighed against more work and responsibility in New York, less service, much less freedom, but something real that I wanted very much. I had been away from America too long. My decision to go back might not have been so easy to make if I hadn't known that, if I did become fashion editor of American *Vogue*, I would return twice a year to cover the collections and to rediscover the streets, the skies, the monuments, the treasures of Paris for which I had a physical love.

Josip Novakovich
ON NOT BEING LATE

While living in Cincinnati, I enjoyed seeing a few tennis matches at the ATP tournament, and in 1994, Goran Ivanišević was going to play, and so I sent a note to the editor of *Tennis Magazine*, the old fashioned way, via stamped mail, that I would like to interview Ivanišević in Croatian to translate into English. As Ivanišević's English was not great, he may have come across unjustly as terse, as someone who didn't have much to say. I suggested that in Croatian he would be more expressive. After all, I could hear him swearing in Croatian after missing a sitter, A jesam ga usra! but I am not going to translate that into English. Moreover, he had the habit of smashing his rackets, and in one tournament he smashed all of his rackets and had to resign the match as he had nothing left to play with. Somebody that temperamental would of course have much to say. So the editor, Jay Jennings (it took me a while now to recall his name, it was so long ago) said, on the phone, I'll send you a press pass. It will come in 3 days, so you'll miss the first day, but he should last, and catch him after the second or third round. I said, sure, I am kind of busy, so I will miss the first round, but I'll catch him deeper into the tournament.

Well, Ivanišević lost round one. No problem, said the editor, in two weeks he will play in Indiana, and I'll pay for your mileage and hotel. It's only like two hours away from Cincinnati?

So I aimed to go to Indianapolis after the second round. Ivanišević was going to last beyond the first round. He was ranked number 3 in the world, and his slip-up in Cincinnati probably had to do with jetlag. Now he was adjusted and he'd do better. But he didn't. He was already out of Indianapolis by the time I got to turn on the ignition key in my old blue Volvo.

— No problem, said the editor. He's playing at the US Open, and I'll send you there. You can fly. I'll set you up in a hotel. But there's no way he won't last a bit longer. Maybe he tanked the tournaments so he'd stay fresh. And the problem with these guys is that they don't like to be distracted in the early rounds, so it's best to try to catch him later on. Who knows, maybe he'll go all the way.

Well, he didn't. He was out after the first round, while I was still checking the ticket prices to NYC.

— You know, this is both frustrating and amusing, said the editor. Tell you what. I'll cover your airfare and three nights of a modest hotel in Paris. You can catch him at the Paris Open, at Bercy. And although I think he will make it further than round one this time, you can go right at the beginning. You know, he won the tournament last year, and he's a defending champion. He'll stand his ground.

Jay never sent me a press pass but said that his letter to me should work, just to show it at the entrance.

I got a hotel, not online, because then very few things were done online, but by walking in the streets near Bastille. The first night I stayed with a friend of mine, Alan, a photographer, whose father was Croatian. His father had committed suicide, and Alan lived in the inherited apartment on the top floor of a four-story building. I walked close to the apartment from the metro, and in a phone booth, dialed his number. Most phones took only magnetic cards, and I had none, but I did find one which took coins. I was not sure how many digits to include and it took me quite a few trials and errors until I finally reached him. He buzzed me in, and I walked up to the fifth floor. Alan welcomed me, his six foot eight frame all dusty. He showed me, he was creating a duplex out of his apartment, by making a staircase into the attic. He said, Nobody in the building must know what I am doing because the property rights about who owns the attic are vague, but if I build it and squat in it a certain amount of time, it's mine.

— What if someone wants to use the attic in the meanwhile, and they find you out?

— I don't know. Maybe I could pay off that person a little to keep quiet.

—That's pretty strange.

— No, you have no idea how expensive real estate has become in

Paris, and this is like warfare, people fighting to get more space. Anyway, I don't have a real job, my photography doesn't pay, and if I pull this one off, I can sell the apartment and buy five in Croatia and live as a landlord and take pictures all day long.

Anyway, a few blocks from his place, I found a two star hotel, and paid for three days. The front desk kept my passport, the old style. The room was small, but no matter. It reminded me of the room I had near Gare du Nord, on my emigration trip to the United States, in 1976, Friday, August 13. I had taken a train to Paris, from where I would fly to New York at 11 in the morning. Exhausted from my trip on the train, I slept till late. I was sure the sun would wake me up early enough, but when I woke up it was so high that I thought it was noon. I rushed downstairs, and it was only 9. I hadn't been used to the Nordic angle of light, nor was I aware of the one hour time difference, which would, coming from the east, give me a slight jetlag in the favor of waking up early. Not to miss the plane, I jumped into a cab, spent nearly all my pocket money for the States, and made it, and everything was fine, except for that moment of panic. Well, now I had a similar panic attack, that Ivanišević would be out already, and I would be late yet again.

It was round two. I got in a little late as it wasn't important to see the whole match, and the guards took a while to scrutinize the letter from Jay Jennings, describing that I was to interview Ivanišević. When I got in, Ivanišević had won the first set comfortably, six three, and was up a game in the second. And then Michael Chang broke his serve, or rather, Ivanišević double faulted, and didn't even smash his racket. Very quickly he lost the second set and then the third. I rushed to the player's lounge, the guards let me through, and I found the father and the son, the Ivaniševićes, sitting at a round table in the dark and drinking Perrier. I introduced myself, and said, Maybe I could have an interview with you?

— Not now. I am not in a good mood, and all I want to do is get back to my hotel and take a shower, a hot one, I've had a cold one here.

— When could I interview you then? You know, it's for *Tennis Magazine*.

— I have no idea, said Goran.

- 211 -

— Maybe tomorrow, come to our hotel at ten in the morning, said his father. I think he'll be in a better mood then. Unless we catch an early flight to Nice.

I called Jay in New York and said, What do you think? What if he doesn't want to talk with me tomorrow and they leave for the airport early?

— Not a problem at all. I'll pay for your flight to Monte Carlo. He's playing in a tournament in five days. Don't you want to see Monte Carlo?

— Sure, but what if things don't work out then either? No, I am just going to his hotel tomorrow and I'll accost him. This is becoming absurd.

— Yes, of course. That could be part of the story. I think it's entertaining already.

— Paris is good enough for me, I said, and we both laughed at my modesty.

I woke up early, showered, had some dismal coffee — why don't the French make coffee as well as the Italians do? The coffee was bitter, and it reminded me of the re-run coffee in the former Yugoslavia, during the shortages, when the coffee operators would pump espresso through the old coffee pack, up to four times. I forgot where I got that coffee, just somewhere near Bastille Circle, near the new Opera House.

I took the blue metro, with those huge rubber wheels buffering the metal, so the ride would be smooth and not overly squeally. I was early, and walked on rue de Rivoli alongside the Louvre. I used to visit the museum, enjoyed the El Grecos and Rembrandts there, but this time I decided, art would not happen. I was now a sports journalist. This is a tougher business, not that aesthetic and sentimental. Art is passé. Next I could probably interview Toni Kukoč. Unfortunately, not Dražen Petrović, who had got killed in a car accident two years before. But perhaps then Davor Šuker, the Croatian soccer player, and when I ran out of Croatian stars, what the hell, I could do the Serbian ones. It might not be all that bad if it involved going to Paris, Madrid, and Chicago. In front of Hotel Intercontinental I saw Pete Sampras, standing on the curb and talking to another man. I looked at him and he looked straight at me and smiled, and so did I; it felt as though I knew him, and of course, I did, from TV, but I didn't say hi, though I was tempted to, and wondered why

I didn't; maybe I could have asked him for an interview too. I was his fan when he played anybody else but Ivanišević. That silent exchange left a good impression on me — what a nice man, I thought. And I wondered, could he figure out I was one of the Balkan dudes on the way to harass Ivanišević? And maybe the smile was an expression of amusement. No matter what, it was relaxed, and he looked genuinely happy.

I walked into the hotel about ten minutes early, and five minutes later, also ahead of schedule, Ivanišević walked from the elevator through the lobby. He wore a brown sweater and looked like a good lanky college lad, a bit taller than I had imagined him. A tu ste, he said. Oh, you are here.

—Yes, I said. If you don't mind, we could just go right to it and I will record our interview. Where should we do it?

— Here is fine. He pointed to two armchairs in the lobby. We sat down, ordered Perriers, and I said, So, a lot of travel. You don't mind that?

— It's fine. I wouldn't have minded a couple more days here, but I messed it up.

— So it was not intentional? I mean, you were so much better than Chang, and just when he looked completely lost, you seemed to lose interest.

— Even if it was intentional, what do you think, that I'd admit it? I don't know what you are going to put into newspapers, but it would be the worst thing to say that a player intentionally blew a tournament, just to go home and get ready for a more important one. I just suddenly lost the momentum and couldn't get it back. Momentum is sometimes a mysterious thing. I don't know how it happened, I am puzzled too.

His voice was deep and he looked very calm, not blinking. He exuded an air of self-confidence. So people talking about what a nervous and neurotic dude he was clearly never sat down with him. The tantrums could be part of a show, a persona on the court, coming from the Ilie Nastase school, but in person, I faced a steady man, a man of powerful will. Well, how else do you get to be in the top 3 in the world in a demanding game that requires a steady hand. I was tempted to ask him to go to a tennis court to serve me a few balls so I could feel what it was like to receive a ball at 140 mph. The max speed in baseball is what, 105? Not much reaction time left. In the meanwhile, I looked past him, and saw Brad Gilbert and Courier. What the fuck? It's so normal here.

We talked for nearly an hour, and I tape recorded it all, and now I would have something to transcribe. I am not going to reproduce the interview which is somewhere in the archives of *Tennis Magazine*, but it's not online, as it was before the everything is online days.

— By the way, at the end I said, could I have three autographs of yours? My nephews in Opatija, I am sure, would love to have your signatures.

— Sure, no problem. We parted like friends. I thought I would see him again. But I didn't have his email address or phone number. I didn't know at the time that I wouldn't actually see him again, certainly not until my writing of this piece, and I don't plan to seek him out.

The interview came out, I got paid 1900 altogether, which in those days was all right, 1000 for expenses, flight and hotel, and the rest, for the honorarium. It could have been more, but I thought, fine, this is my entry level. And what if I had gone on to Monte Carlo? That would have been perhaps one grand more. And I would have perhaps seen the casinos, a setting for the *Confession of a Murderer* by Joseph Roth, and for many movies.

The interview done, I took the metro back to the hotel, and realized I had enough time to visit a few graves at Père Lachaise, only a few stops east of Bastille. I walked in a new section near the crematorium, and an old woman with hairs all white looked at me, and asked, Vous cherchez Proust? She pointed — three rows down, and one to the left and voila! How the hell did she know I was looking for Proust? At least I knew, no matter what, I would not be too late to find him. Nobody was going to chase him out of Paris to Monte Carlo. Our silent interview could take place at our time, his and mine, and if not this time, then another, but always only at Père Lachaise.

Peter Selgin
FROM A PARIS NOTEBOOK

Paris, 12 Aout, 199 —

At an outdoor table at a café on the Boulevard Diderot ("Men will never be free until the last king is strangled to death with the entrails of the last priest"). Cane chairs, Gitane smoke, the Gare de Lyon across the street. I'm reminded of something. Twenty-three years ago, when I was nineteen, I slept there, in the station. I took off my shoes and curled up on a luggage cart. I woke up to find myself rolling under girders, a pair of porters laughing as they trundled me. That same morning I begged patrons at café tables like this one for their uneaten croissants.

Jean jacket, cowboy boots, scruffy beard.

My first trip to Europe.

Waiting for Josiane, who wants to take me to some museums.

•

Josiane and I met at the top of the gorge, where she straddled her *vélo*. I spent three weeks there, in Bozouls, at an artist's residency at the base of the eight-hundred foot gorge, living in one of two stone towers guarding the walled village. I had my own yard and a table for my watercolors. My sponsor, an international lawyer, was suddenly called to New York City on an important case. I knew no one in the village. I was completely on my own there.

The next day Josiane drove us to the public pool in Espallion, where the night before for 4F apiece we watched the fireworks display from the candle-lit bridge. When we arrived at the pool I discovered I'd left my *maillot* back at the tower. I raided the lost-and-found box for a substitute, settling on a polka-dotted Speedo that Josiane found *"très drôle."*

•

Tristan and Gregoire, Josiane's grown sons, the products of different failed marriages, met us there. I raced them across the fifty-meter pool, to a dead heat with Gregoire, though Tristan beat us both easily.

"Let's do a hundred!" I said.

Josiane exercised on the lawn. For a woman with two strapping triathlete sons, she's in terrific shape, firm and muscular, with marvelous upthrust breasts.

•

In Bozouls it rained almost every day, a bleak atmosphere that mimicked the colors of the stone houses and walls. Women in dark shawls carried wicker baskets of dried fruit; wiry men in dusty work clothes playing boules; church bells tolling in the damp air; desultory faces glimpsed through stone windows; a man burning twigs in his yard, another splitting wood, a third wielding a pick-axe against a pile of stones ... Waiflike children crowding around my café table, saying, "What are you writing? What are you sketching? Write about me. Draw *my* picture!"

And though I enjoyed my solitude, climbing up and down the steep road to one of two cafes on the lip of the gorge, writing and sketching in my journal while sipping coffee or an aperitif and watching the sun go up or down, I was lonesome.

After three weeks all those gray stones depressed me.

I longed for museums and pretty women. I longed for Paris.

•

I've been sitting outdoors, sun-stroked, sipping my *citron pressé,* when from the darkness inside a voice calls to me.

Josiane! She's been sitting there all the time.

"I never sit in the sun," she says. "Never!"

She wears a black dress, with a gold and silver necklace, her hair Henna-dyed a deep purple. We exchange the customary triple-kiss, more customary in the country than here in Paris, where, Josiane tells me, people are more *fermés*, more closed.

"Paris isn't the city of love they say it is," she warns me. "It is a city of lonely, sullen, arrogant people."

•

In her car we ride to the center of Paris. By the Place de Clichy we park and cross the bridge spanning the cemetery where Truffaut, Berlioz, Stendhal, Soutine, Sartre, de Beauvoir, Baudelaire, Brancusi, Maupassant, Beckett, Jim Morrison, and Jean Seberg are buried.

From there we walk to Montmartre, of Paris' thirteen *collines* the only one of any amplitude, Montparnasse being but a gentle swell, though none of the hills is large enough to prevent the city from looking, from atop the Eiffel Tower, like a pancake.

•

Montmartre: home to bad art and the Sacré Coeur, crowning the hill with its dozen breast-like white domes. For 1.5 F you can enjoy a snack while taking in the view from which the Eiffel Tower, hidden by trees, is conspicuously absent.

Having taken (and failed) Josiane's snap geography quiz, I stroll with her down the twisting cobblestone streets immortalized by Gene Kelly, finding them strangely empty. Tourists, mimes, postcard racks. A mime done up as the Statue of Liberty but in white greasepaint.

We turn corners, swinging past what's said to have been Dali's studio, but is actually a small water tower with very narrow windows. Then down a flight of steep stone stairs up which a man in a suit, smoking a pipe and looking very much like Georges Simenon, ascends.

•

"Petit Musée de Montmartre." Modesty being so rare, we decide to have a look. The fee isn't so modest, 40F per person, nor are the proprietors inclined to underestimate the worth of their holdings, or the public's willingness to make off with them. I'm forced to check a plastic shopping bag — unhappily, since it holds my notebook, my glasses, and a box of sketching pens.

Muttering something to the effect that I doubt I could fit any of their precious relics in my little bag, I stuff its contents into various pockets.

●

Small though it is, the collection was worth the price of admission, with paintings, sketches, letters and other documents by Utrillo, Andre Utter, Max Jacob, posters by Lautrec and Vlaminck, and a room where the bar at Café de l'Abreuvoir, Utrillo's favorite watering hole, has been reconstituted bottle by bottle, complete with zinc sink and silver absinthe spoons.

Though I don't steal anything, there are things in the little museum I'd like to steal, including several small paintings and watercolors by Redon, Derain, and my favorite, Rouault, whose portrait of two judges consists of a series of slashed lines of thick black ink snaring swatches of dazzling color.

Next to the Rouault, in a sickly diploma frame that does it no justice, a letter from Max Jacob to Maurice Raynal at the bottom of which a figure in blue ink emerges from a ghostly filigree of the most gorgeous handwriting. What I'd give to have handwriting like that! I'd never stop writing. I'd be a graphomaniac.

As we step from one small room into the next, my eyes grow wider, my heart beats faster. Letters, poems, notebook pages and other documents by Apollinaire, Modigliani, van Dongen, and Pascin, old menus from the Dome and the Rotonde, a paint box, a pencil holder, a pocket watch, a pair of silk gloves …

The Valium I swallowed aboard the night train from Toulouse has worn off. I've forgotten all about the woman with whom I'd shared my *wagon-lit*. I've even forgotten all about Josiane, who stands here next to me — not so much about her, as about the prospect of sex with her — a prospect that has scented the air all morning long with a trace of *eau de toilette,* but that fades as I gaze into the sultry haze spreading itself over the slums of Paris that we stand facing together.

Meanwhile Josiane points out yet another architectural wonder that, for all I care, could be the Great Pyramid of Giza or Yankee Stadium. They could build another Eiffel Tower in front of us, for all I care.

All that matters to me at the moment is art: Max Jacob's art, Utrillo's art, Rouault's art, but mostly my own art, whatever form it might take in the near future. For the first time in weeks I feel inspired.

•

I forgot my little plastic bag, the one in which I'd carried my notebook, my glasses, my pen box, walking out of the Petit Musée de Montmartre without it. When I returned for it, the receptionist looked at me over the tops of her bifocals as if I were a rare specimen of insect. "Your *leetle* bag is over there," she said in sniffy, precise English, pointing with her elongated chin to the corner.

"*Merci,*" I said, taking a step toward it.

"You know," she added in French, smiling, "the little bag which you so cleverly remarked is too small to steal anything in this museum. Hmm?"

"Yes, thank you," I said, returning her smile while reaching for it.

"As you no doubt have observed, *monsieur,*" she added while pretending to be preoccupied with something else, something more important, "our museum, small and relatively obscure though it may be, holds many priceless items which might very well fit into your small and, incidentally, rather unprepossessing bag."

"Uh, yes, indeed," I said, and started to leave. By this time the lady had withdrawn from under the counter a lethal looking knife, a *Laguiole* like the ones Josiane collected, with a handle of ox horn, or was it tortoise shell? With a flourish she popped out the serrated blade. It caught the harsh light of the vestibule. I wondered if she intended to slit my insolent American throat with it.

"You see this knife?" she asked, carving a square shape into the air before my eyes. "Two slices — *comme ça* — *!*" another square, " — and a document worth 100,000 … 200,000 … 300,000 francs — more! — *et voilà:* out of the frame it goes and into a small, ugly, plastic bag such as yours."

"You're so right, Madame," I said, and holding my bag tentatively, as if it contained either a priceless relic or a lump of *merde,* I started out of the museum again. But madam wasn't through with me.

"And if you think it hasn't happened, *monsieur,* think again! It has, several times! Only last month a man such as yourself, a foreigner, an American (she spat the word) left here with two — *two!* — small etchings of Vlaminck — *oui, monsieur,* in a plastic bag — one no larger than yours!" She waved the *Laguiole* menacingly at me and my plastic bag that, were it not for that knife, I'd have used to suffocate her. "So you see, monsieur, just how *stupide* was your remark, *oui?"*

Parisians, so critical yet so thin-skinned. The thing to do in cases like this is to humble oneself. Two things Parisians respond well to: insults and groveling. Nothing in-between will suffice.

"Madame," I say, "You are so right. But then I'm just a loutish American tourist. What do I know of art, of museums, of thieves — of plastic bags? Forgive my insolence and ignorance. As long as I live, I shall never attempt to enter a museum of any kind with a small, plastic bag. Certainly not your museum, Madam, which I shall remember — along with you — for the rest of my days."

●

The thing about journals: you have to be honest in them. There's no point lying. Tell one lie in the pages of a journal and everything in it turns to shit.

No place for secrets in a notebook.

Who writes these words? A man-child in Paris, a man who looks at himself in reflective surfaces, who picks his nose, who reads himself to sleep, who suffers insomnia and untold headaches, who prefers wine to beer, who finds men and women equally attractive, but sleeps only with women; who, in a pinch, will use anyone's toothbrush, who eats buttered toast that has fallen on the floor, who hates flossing, who sneezes as loudly as he possibly can, who masturbates frugally, as if someone were keeping track, who likes striped socks, who never balances his checkbook, who hates the thought of growing old, who thinks the whole world should be a café, or maybe a library, or maybe both — with a lake or ocean nearby (who once swam in a lake with a cafe beside it, literally stripped to his Speedo in the bathroom and came out and dove into the lake with his cappuccino still warm on the table) … whose handwriting is godawful, whose drawing pens tend to leak, who draws like an angel and flirts like the devil, who has trouble believing in anything, who can't stand bare walls, who finds it too warm, who deplores the color "beige," who has turned into his father in spite of everything, whose hair refuses to turn gray, who used to sing, who finds anchovies divine, who takes the Lord's name in vain, who is increasingly nearsighted, who favors one leg, whose fingers are small vis-à-vis his palms, who will never find perfect silence, whose dreams, when he has them, aren't the least bit memorable, who really should buy a decent pair of shoes, who finishes other people's sentences, whom timorous people find arrogant (a perception owing as much to their timorousness as to his arrogance), who fears strictly heterosexual men, especially those near to him in age, who forgets to drink water, who detests forced joy as expressed by the ejaculation *whoopie,* who thinks neckties should be worn by the homeless, who considers diet Coca-Cola a vast conspiracy, who from time to time, still, but more and more rarely as he grows older, laments having given up becoming a movie star …

Then again it's impossible to ever know anyone, really.

•

From Montmartre we descend through a square jammed with tourist stalls of bad art, palette paintings of "quaint" Parisian streets, faux Utrillos, Pissarros and Dufys … Seeing so much bad art makes me famished for the real thing. I especially long to see an original by Louis Vivin, whose paintings I fell in love with when I chanced upon one in a book about naive artists. Like *Le Douanier* Rousseau, Vivin was a former postal clerk who spent his pension years painting. Unlike Rousseau, Vivin worked not from imagination, but from postcards, producing dogmatically literal paintings of Parisian monuments — the Louvre, the Pantheon, Sacré Coeur, Notre Dame — devotional paintings in which nearly every trace of perspective is obliterated while every last brick and window is accounted for with a child's obsessive earnestness. Vivin's guileless canvasses are permeated with his innocent joy. They conjure a calm structured world wherein humans and buildings exist in perfect order and harmony, a world where such things as wars, poverty, and disaster don't exist, and life is a monument to itself. Vivin's paintings are so utterly void of irony or cynicism, looking at them may increase one's appetite for reality. And yet there's nothing realistic about Vivin's paintings, which in their stubborn literalness rub up against surrealism.

And though he stands by every brick and window, Vivin takes joyful liberties with his colors, turning bricks and sidewalks pink, skies yellow, windows blue, roofs ocher, and cobblestones the dusty purple of a storm at sea.

•

We drive past the boutiques of St. Germain, to a district of specialty shops and galleries in the 7th *arrondisement,* in search of *Le Fondation Dina Vierny,* where the *Musee Maillol* is located, and where Josiane — who like all Parisians knows her art — says they have a large collection of primitive and naïve works, including some Vivins. But when we get there the gallery is holding an exhibition on a contemporary sculptor, its permanent holdings in storage. There is, however, a bookshop where I find a monograph of Louis Vivin's work, brimming with color plates and costing a mere 295 francs — a steal.

The book under my arm we repair to a nearby café, where I flip the pages. Josiane approves of Vivin's art, her Vanessa Redgrave smile widening with each color plate. We go through the whole book, arriving at last at a photograph of the artist. With its buffoonish mustache, Vivin's is indeed the face of a former postal official: dull, dim, officious — the kind of face children poke fun at.

"*Il n'est pas beau,*" Josiane observes.

"*Au contraire. Il est trés beau.*" For me, at that moment, Louis Vivin is the handsomest man in the world.

•

I've no idea what Josiane does for a living, among other things, and know better than to ask. In general the French don't like to talk about work, and Parisians in particular are cagey when it comes to their vocations, especially if the inquiring party is a New Yorker. Unlike New Yorkers, Parisians aren't career-obsessed; given a choice they'd much rather live than work. They don't much care what they do, provided it allows them ample time for lunch and vacations.

●

Our free admission to the *Musee d'Art Moderne* entitles us only to the Dufy and Matisse rooms. "La Fée Électricité," the huge mural Dufy designed for the 1937 *Exposition Internationale*, is there in its entirety. Dufy's paintings always annoy me slightly, with their willful sloppiness and the way the color patches in the background bump into one another in sickly ways. Dufy disdains slickness. That said, a lot of his work, certainly "La Fée Électricité" (commissioned by the French equivalent of Con Ed), is illustrative. Whether his work is illustrative or not, Dufy discovered a magical language of line and color that's as elegant and simple as a picnic on the beach, or Chinese calligraphy. His paintings are really sketches, blown-up jottings from the artist's notebook, elevated — through fearlessness and craft — to masterpieces.

●

Matisse's *La Danse de Paris* covers the upper third of a long white wall. A half-dozen bloated gray figures with arms and legs cropped, victims of a grisly murder dredged from the Seine — dance against a background of scumbled blue. Unlike Dufy, Matisse was clearly uninterested in prettiness. Even his most decorative works seldom put one in mind — as Dufy's often do — of wallpaper.

As for *La Danse de Paris,* I've got to say, it works its magic on me, with its subtle blues and grays dancing next to a sly border of sepia-brown. How does an artist arrive at such color harmonies — sepia-brown against gray and blue? Succulent! And all those minute variations in color, that tiny blot of pacific cobalt, for instance, in a restless sea of slate blue. And those dozens of shades of gray — gray, my all-time favorite color, since it's impossible, since there's no such color, there can *be* no such color, just as there's no such thing as black or white, only the concept of blackness or the absence of light — the absence of seeing — an absence that makes all colors *impossible*. Which is why gray is my favorite color, since it mixes the impossibility of *black* with the impossibility of *white* (all colors of absolute intensity combined absolutely), creating a third impossibility, the ultimate impossibility: *Gray*. And people think gray's a dull color! *La Danse de Paris* is a feast, a smorgasbord in serene blue and impossible gray, colors not happy or sad, that make something like joy out of something like despair.

•

The most interesting sight at the Musée D'Orsay is the building, the former Gare d'Orsay, rendered obsolete as a train station by the construction of the Gare Montparnasse. Parisians have a favorite poster, a historic photograph of a locomotive that has just rammed through an outer wall of the Gare d'Orsay.

The inscription: "Merde."

•

Picasso is a barrel of monkeys — and rhinos and toucans and elephants and bulls and fish and sunny women with assholes where their hearts should be. He made guitars from rusty tin cans and goats out of hat blocks and rope. Hating Picasso is like hating a child. Deplore Picasso and you deplore human nature.

Picasso is Picasso because he's free, and he's free because he's Picasso.

I used to not like Picasso all that much. I thought he was a clever painter who imitated other artists, who stole their ideas and ran with them faster than any of them could run. Then, when he got tired of them, he'd drop them and seek out other amusements.

That's what I used to think. Now I think pretty much the same thing, with this difference: now I consider him a genius, an innovator and not just an imitator. As good a painter as he was (and he was pretty good), he was an even better liberator. Picasso gave permission to Art. Like a lifeguard performing artificial resuscitation on a drowning victim, he breathed lust and vigor into its deflated, waterlogged lungs. "From now on," he decided, "a painting can be, among other things, ugly." And he unveiled his *Demoiselles.*

Having given paintings permission to be "ugly," Picasso made ugly paintings beautiful. He made ugly paintings so beautiful that for the next half century other artists banged their heads into walls and tied themselves into knots trying to figure out how to make ugly paintings ugly again.

•

Fed up with museums, we cross the boulevard to a café, where, over *salades de Roquefort,* Josiane fills me in on her past loves. As unwilling as they are to discuss work, Parisians are more than happy, eager even, to talk about love. She has quite a history, Josiane, with men and women young and old, including several encounters with people she met on her *vélo,* one a parking lot attendant.

"What next?" I say when we've finished our meal.

"*Comme tu veux.*"

It's her answer to everything. If I said, "Let's cross the city in a hot air balloon," or "Let's get married," Josiane would say, "*Comme tu veux.*"

•

We speed past *fleuristes* and *bouquinistes* along the Quai de la Mégisserie, headed for the Cluny baths. Parisian streets defy logic, neither parallel nor perpendicular, but at odd angles, while changing course two or three times, so halfway down a one-way street you find yourself going the wrong way.

By the time we leave the baths it's four thirty. There's a cinema across the street. "Allons," says Josiane, taking my arm.

•

Venus in Fur, the movie, shot in black and white, is about a sadomasochistic relationship. Lingering shots of wax dripping from a lit candle onto a woman's nipple; a man on all fours with a stiletto heel hovering over the small of his back.

I've never seen the appeal of masochism or sadism. Combining them only doubles my distaste. There's something silly about people playing with pain, as if it were a kid's box of colored crayons.

As for mixing it with pleasure, it's like putting ketchup on a truffle omelet, or playing Mozart's *Requiem* at the wrong speed.

But the movie grips Josiane, who's seen it several times, making me wonder if she's got a thing for nipple clamps and cigarette burns. Am I being initiated? Does she keep whips in her bookcase, with her Robbe-Grillet novels and her collection of *Laguiole* knives, including her favorite with the tri-colored handle — feldspar, azurite, and marble — the colors of the French flag?

Question: What did the sadist say to the masochist? Answer: No.

•

Back in Josiane's Fiat, streaming along the Marne toward her neighborhood and a restaurant antipathetic to tourists. She points to a bridge stained with twilight.

"There is where I cross the river on my *vélo*," she says. "And there — " she points again, " — is where I took a nasty spill on my *vélo* three years ago and nearly split my skull. And there, by those four big trees, one day on my *vélo* …"

It emerges that Josiane has lived much of her life, grown up, been educated, worked, fallen in love, lost her virginity, been married thrice and spawned two strapping athletic offspring — all on her *vélo*. I'm reminded of a game played with Chinese fortune cookies in which the phrase "in bed" is added to the end of every fortune, but in Josiane's case the words are *on my vélo*.

"And there — " She points yet again, each thrust of her finger stabbing my tired, hungry brain. "That's where I met my third husband, Claude, *on my vélo*."

•

At an Italian bistro in Saint-Maur we eat a pizza named after Romeo and Juliet. The *patron* looks like Louis Vivin. He practices his Italian on me. *"Allora, come ti piace la mia pizza?"* From her purse Josiane unfolds a photocopied *pièce de théâtre* by Peter Handke. Together we translate it into English:

Play the game. Threaten work (?) Don't be the main event. Seek out confrontation, yet have no intentions. Do away with hindsight. Don't keep things to yourself. Be soft yet strong. Be clever. Jump in but despise victory. Don't observe, don't examine, but be alert to the signs, be vigilant. Be shakable. Show your eyes, lead others into profundity, give them their space and consider each in his own image. Make choices only out of enthusiasm. Crash calmly. Above all take your time and take detours. Let yourself be distracted. Take yourself, so to speak, on a vacation. Don't neglect the sound of a single tree, or a single river. Go where you desire and give yourself the sun. Forget your family, give strength to strangers, embrace details. Go where there's no one, ignore destiny, disdain sadness, appease conflict with your smile. Be colorful and be within your rights, such that the sound of leaves turns sweet. Pass through the villages — I'll follow you.

•

Naturally I want to sleep with her, but I don't want to presume. Nor do I want to go back to my one-star hotel, with its coughs and bells.

I'm reminded of something a friend once told me about Parisian women, how their attitude toward sex is infinitely more relaxed than in the U.S., how the average Parisian views sex more-or-less as we Americans view a glass of water. You offer it to anyone who looks thirsty.

•

Like most Parisians Josiane lives far from the city center, in a cramped studio in a stucco building in a less-than-enchanting neighborhood. Clean, though, and quiet, stocked with experimental literature and avant-garde music in glassed-in cases.

I watch her squat in front of an old-fashioned tape recorder, the kind with two big plastic reels, threading Strauss's Four Last Lieders through its rollers and capstans.

The constipation tablets work. As we lay stretched out on her sofa listening to the fourth lieder I hear the sound of the distant cavalry, followed by a minor earthquake occurring somewhere in a neglected island nation below the equator.

In Josiane's bathroom — as cramped and sparkling as the rest of her home — the world empties out of me: Romeo, Juliet, wine, dreams, doubts, desires, regrets, Dufy, Redon, Vivin, Sacré Coeur, Le Petit Musée de Montmartre, ambitions, promises, Rouault, Picasso, and so forth. Kettledrum hollow, I emerge.

●

With Vivaldi's *Stabat Mater* playing on her anachronistic tape recorder, under her bookshelves sagging with *nouveaux romans,* her hennaed hair showing traces of gray at the roots, her breasts tasting bitterly of perfume, the muscles of her *derrière en poire* so solid the eyes on the moth wings tattooed there scarcely flutter with our thrusts, we make uncomplicated love. While thrusting away I'm thinking *it's impossible, we'll never really know each other. She is darkness personified!*

Afterwards I fall into a deep sleep, waking minutes later to the buzz of an electric saw. It's pitch dark. Some shithead is sawing wood. With an electric saw. At two o'clock in the morning. *On a Sunday!*

"That is Jacques, my neighbor," Josiane explains, yawning. "He is putting a new floor on his terrace."

"Est-il fou?" ("Is he insane?")

"Pourquoi?"

"Does he know what time it is?"

"I am certain that he does."

"It's two o'clock in the morning!"

Josiane laughs. "You are wrong. It is my windows. The blinds — they are *hermetic* ("air-meh-teek"). Look!"

She leaps out of bed, flies to her window, pulls open the blinds.

In pours the sunshine of a late Sunday afternoon.

Philip Kobylarz
IN MEROVINGIA

Arrival

The airport is crowded, voice from overhead, louder than necessary, singing phrases that cannot be understood, except for the names of places: Amsterdam, Rabat, Stuttgart, Algiers, Madrid, Paris, Dakar. It could be an airport in any major city in the world, yet there are subtleties of difference/definition. Near the bathroom, a woman waits seated at a table, furniture dated by a once modern aerospace style: mid rocket years sixties. She has what appears to be an ashtray barely filled with coins in front of her. She is not smoking. Sometimes, she opens her paperback and takes a glance. Mostly, she sits staring vacantly into the distance, not even hearing the *toilettes* flushing behind her, the dull murmur of plumbing constantly cleansing itself. She is waiting for a tip, for a few coins that the release from a bodily function is worth these days. Usually not much, a franc or two. Never a paper bill. Never too much.

It is time to catch the connecting flight. Nearly a half an hour before it is to take off, passengers are queuing for seats. The line, at first modeled loosely on the British form — straight with ample elbowroom — soon, as the countdown begins, erodes into a flimsy semi-circle. The intelligent — spawns of a survival of the fittest process — begin to sneak in on either side of the semi-circle, towards the entrance gate. White-haired men are seen zipping small dogs into carry-on bags, not taking the time to make sure they don't catch the dog's curly hair in the seam. Copies of *Le Monde* or *Le Provençal* are hastily tucked under arms. The concept of personal space is all but obliterated: people stand on each other's heels, elbows connect with sides; humid after meal breath is shared, anonymous line-standers become almost intimate with one another, scents of perfume are exchanged, yet no one is pushed to the point of painful discomfort or even the threshold of anger. This is just the way the machine works. Conversation about the weather and the ineptitude of airline personnel breaks out sporadically. Cigarettes are extinguished at the last breath, the last second. Through a cloud of exhaled tobacco, you enter France.

TANGENTIAL

Escape the confusion of flight numbers that add up to their own trigonometry with no solutions and slip into the city that is much too far from the airport. The fields that surround are flat and mildly undulating, as fields should be, a haze hangs over them to suggest the mystery that lies beyond. On the bus into the city, the people are well dressed and as silent as mutes. Passing through over- and under- passes, then into the preliminary maze of the outskirts, trash of a different nature lines the road side. Occasionally, there are pieces of habitations: light fixtures, fenders of outdated automobiles, racks from refrigerators, lampshades, then paper refuse of products that a third world country can only dream of: brightly colored garbage as decoration. It occurs to one that this country, like other fantastically rich countries, has too much to throw away.

The body heat within the bus fogs the windows, obscuring views of places that don't want to be seen anyway. The silence on the bus is reverence for the hard, lonely work of travel.

ENTER, THE LABYRINTH

> *Maintenant tu marches dans Paris tout seul*
> *parmi la foule / Des troupeaux d'autobus*
> *mugissants près de toi roulent / L'angoisse de*
> *l'amour te serre le gosier / Comme si tu ne*
> *devais jamais plus être aimé*
>
> —Apollinaire

Paris is a monument to itself. A monument constantly building and rebuilding its own glory. Its busiest and most remarkable streets, Boulevard St. Michel, Saint Germain des Prés, are filled with steady lines of people skirting around crews of road repairmen. The bowels of the street are exposed for all to see. Rubble, dirt, rocks — why plaster of Paris is named so. Pipes coming from and returning to their respective circles of hell. Absent is the smell, feel, texture of asphalt: here the streets and the buildings are, for the most part, real. Made of the stuff that they have always been made of. Made of concrete, stone, marble, dirt, materials that the sense of touch desires. This is no Michigan Avenue where the monstrosities that surround are of unimaginable glass and steel welded together into canyons of inhumanity that mock nature. Trees here aren't belittled by their surroundings: they are, within the realms of their little wrought iron fences, an integral part of the city. Bird apartments. Parks, within the city, crop up unexpectedly and offer a refuge of vegetation and real earth underfoot. They are also gathering places for those seeking refuge within refuge: people *peuple* them — reading books, lovers sit on each other's lap inspecting their reflection in each other's eyes, the homeless sleep on their benches undisturbed, pigeons decorate them as if they are about to break into a game of pétanque. They aren't the tools for guided amusement, swings, seesaws, as they are in the States. Here, their inhabitants know what to do in city parks: breathe, relax, sit, see, be. Do absolutely nothing.

The apartment buildings that surround these green spaces, are, on a human scale, gigantic. Rows and rows of shutters, mostly closed, but in the months of summer, wide open. They reveal backdrops of horrendous wallpaper, beautiful antique armoires or bureaus, lines of laundry hanging from tiny perches of porches, odd light fixtures retained due to function more than aesthetic. The oddest aspect: there are millions of these decorated caves, filled with strange and wonderful people who have not opted for life in the new American-style suburbs that unfortunately exist, those who cling to the myth of the city and populate it with their belief in the grandiosity of it all. The rents, apparent to all from pastings in windows of real estate agents (as if they were a type of coveted pastry), are explosively high. Apartments with terraces, or at least, rooms of differing levels, are worth a child's weight in silver. The views from them garner every penny spent. Seen from within the city, the city reveals its very brainwork, its interior, clockwork of its architecture, an exploded inside view. Inhabitants bear with the impossible task of parking, the crowded métros, grocery stores packed with hungry rummagers at a preordained shopping time, just to live the monuments of their lives in a monument to life: the greatest city ever achieved.

STREETS

Appropriately called rues, they contain a certain sadness, the kind embodied in great works of art. The Mona Lisa's plaintive smile, the gloom of Redon's etchings color these traverses and alleys. The bizarrity of Atget's project comes into light. Why a man would spend a lifetime photographing block after block of mere passageways and buildings becomes clear only upon visitation of the scene. The beauty of the city's arterial street system often escapes a black and white, matter of fact real time presentation. The immense layering of humanity is lost, unless stumbled upon, followed within. Around every corner, a new discovery is to be made.

Kiosks stand like obelisks centering a place or pinpointing a corner. Covered in a skin of past and present events, they seem to be molting themselves of happenings: concerts, lectures, circuses, calls for auditions, ways in which to be assimilated deeper into the buildings and life that surrounds. More numerous than their sheets of glossy sheaves are the millions of staples sunk into their wooden planks, like eyeteeth multiplying. One cannot pass a kiosk without looking at it, or touching. They are the un-peopled sentries of the streets patiently waiting to ring out the news for those who have the time, or interest, to connect. They are polyglots, offering conversation in Vietnamese, English, Arabic, Russian, incorrect French. They repel with their banal vulgarity: the telephone sex number of a posing half-nude named Yaya or Mimi revealing a flank of thigh and two crescents of nipples. This is most naturally pasted next to a multi-color poster of a coming concert of Rimski-Korsakov. Two sides of the same coin in the city of any desire.

Another trinket of the past that characterizes the interior — *pissoires*. Not the automated pay toilets that look like construction worker johns on the moon, but green painted metal mock Calders that stand as drones. Private pillboxes. What these are actually needed for can't be simply explained. A man here hasn't the slightest hesitation in pulling his vehicle over to the side of the road and pissing one step from his car door. Or, as a pedestrian, bee lining to the nearest bush or semi-darkened doorway, to relieve himself in a stream of eternity. They must serve as relics of medieval days, when walkways served as sewers; or perhaps reminders of the war: singular Maginot lines, tiny bunkers unto themselves, where the army of quotidian life can enter a coat of armor, peer through the small window-holes, and release a singular cannon with hardly even having to aim. In the months of summer, the *pissoires* add to the humid flavor of the streets, adding a different brand of stench to the air, which is characteristically unlike the bad water aftertaste of New York's waterfront or the smell within the drained swamp skyscraper park on either side of the Chicago River. The structures are painted green — to suggest vegetation? To be inconspicuous? Whatever the motive, their existence in scent and color says it all.

LANDSCAPE

Countryside. That which is outside of city, undulating planes of green, stands of trees, is, by suggestion, portrayed accurately in clouds of daybreak, sunset. In this city that dazzles the eye with its multi-fold inventions and re-inventions of architecture, the sky goes unnoticed. Rarely is there enough empty space to tempt a viewer to look up. A crook in the neck from walking too much in one day will do. Above, shape shifters: white, grey, backgrounds of pink, yellow, or the usual blue.

What is particular about Paris is the ornamentation it provides for its already remarkable river Seine. Nowhere in America is there a river so brazenly decorated. Not even along its sister the Mississippi. No New Orleans, Memphis, or Minneapolis celebrates its arterial flow as the quays, the embankments, the islands of Paris do. The result of this appreciation of water as destination is found in the annoying bateaux-mouches that light up the nighttime flow, and encase buildings in spotlights, as if they are in the process of mining for tourist attractions. In the U.S., there are riverboat cruises on historical paddle boats, but the focus of these trips is to internalize the pleasures of the river's freedom by providing such distractions as "fine" dining and low stakes gambling. In Paris, to see the city from a boat is to become a platelet within the blood flow. The *Ile de la Cité* is a microcosm of the metaphor of Paris: encircled by placidity, a structure of greatness, of pomp, residing to mark the spot of a coming together and resting and realization that you are somewhere and the resulting beauty of it and of your realization. Celtic tribes. Romans. Their descendants. Invading barbarians. A mingling of a certain Gallic jumble of it all.

The larger parks of the city are sculptured, mainly by the years and ensuing history, into gathering places somewhere in between civilization and the wild. There are hardly any momentous forms of nature, although some buttes do remain, and in the places of loping hills, kept and unkempt gardens, lawns of sensuous grass, man's attempt to comment upon, invade, or tame these oases is ever present. That the word butte, used in the American West to ordinate square erosional plugs of mountains, comes from the French word to describe a hill built to absorb target-shot bullets: *butte de tir, but:* goal. But in America we've already killed nature off enough so we rifle highway signs. Deconstruction of the final metaphor. Manifest Density.

Here, hills have a Zen-like quality and style: Romanesque columns rise from a pond, Italianate bridges hop a stream, triumphal arches erode among husks of tree trunks years older than their manmade partners. Something like the contemplative quality of the monument park in Washington D.C. with its Japanese cherries and Greek revival architecture, a tranquil zone like this is usually overlooked as a non-walkable banality. But then that capitol was designed by a Frenchman. In eternal balance: humanity's dual nature; one angelic, one wild; as represented in the plans these parks carve out of the earth, the rocks, the vegetal consciousness that is already there. And will be after we are long gone.

Sewers of Paris

Are underground; the glory underneath the glory. Filled with the bones of Egyptians, of captured mummies, of broken, stolen obelisks. They contain stashes of great art hidden by departing Nazis. Reenactments of Roman catacombs, with buried treasures, vases, statuettes, wall paintings done by nomadic Etruscans. Are the bowels of the city filtering the spore-filled waste of the world's best food and wine, processed into bile, a rich pâté of fertilizer. Are built with the monoliths of druids. Concentrically circle the great town leading down to a Plutonic cesspool of regeneration. Provide getaways for the Wanted, including the cave-like abode Jack the Ripper inhabited in his last, miserable, rat-like years of existence. Lead to secret bunkers where the armies of France, and her many Kings and Emperors concealed treasures earned in victory: golden samovars, a jade-studded crown of a caliph, the first horologe (made of silver and ivory), an original copy, in gold leaf and camel leather, of the Koran.

DEPARTURE

Rue Haute-des-Ursins. Impasse des Provençaux. Rue Beurrière. Rue Jacinthe. Place d'Enfer. Have all disappeared, physically, or by name. In this city, streets, through history, have acted as revolving doors. They have been built upon, or continued into different places from the ones they had once been. Their existences have been recorded in photographs (see Atget and Marville) and literature: Henry Miller, Orwell, Baudelaire, to mention three drops in the bucket. More so than the monuments of Invalides or Notre-Dame, the Dome of *Sacré Coeur,* the myth of the Left Bank, the streets of Paris will tempt you to return.

Even though you can still go to the cobbled streets of Montmartre and find an enclosed square of artists painting landscapes and portraits, artists who will take your seventy dollars (conveniently located on the square is a money changing office) and after they share some words with you in English, Italian, or German, will head into the local bar to make good on a tab, or begin another. Art eternally inspiring itself.

Even though you can still amble through the city to the gate of *Père Lachaise* and get lost in the city within a city of tombs and hauntingly beautiful burial sites and, at the grave of Chopin or Apollinaire, find freshly cut flowers and people in silence, in awe, visiting, paying respects, this will serve as an experience enough to never be repeated.

Even though you can play tourist and visit the horrendous *Beaubourg,* escalating up its tubular exoskeleton to find a joke of an eatery at the top with food priced as if there were a siege taking place below, yet beyond it, a spectacular view of the city in mid-afternoon haze, with domes and spires silhouetting the beyond as an invitation to try and find, within the maze, their buried foundations, you will snap a few photos, stand spellbound at its entrance square, upon departure, to watch the few odd street musicians play their tunes, juggle bowling pins, or preach about the end of the world. And the invention of others.

Always awaiting are the streets, the one true glory of the city, to take you back to your hotel, in style, with enchantment, flowing with ever present water and the rags of the *cantonnier* in the gutters, alive with refuse, empty wine bottles, spit, the footfalls of millions of people like you who came here to find the secret of Paris, who unknowingly cross over it, step upon it, drive through it, for eternity, everyday. City of lights. No, city of rues.

Liane Kupferberg Carter
LICKING THE WINDOWS

After the initial euphoria of booking a trip to Paris for our upcoming 30th anniversary, sobering reality sets in.

My husband Marc sends an email to our lawyer. "This is a major leap of faith for us," he writes. "We have never left Mickey at home with care givers for so long and flown so far away. We are still hyperventilating thinking about it. That being said, we would like to have our wills and new trusts fully executed before we leave."

All parents think of these things. But when you have a developmentally disabled young adult son at home, you feel a particular urgency.

The idea of an anniversary trip started last month when, over the Presidents' Week school break, my sister-in-law, my cousin, their teenage daughters and I took a girls' trip to Paris. I kept sending Marc excited text messages and photos: Notre Dame, dazzling against a dusky night sky; a polychromatic pasta display at Le Bon Marché; a *bateau mouche,* slipping beneath a floodlit bridge. And chocolate. Chocolate shops seemingly everywhere. I was mesmerized by the exquisite windows jammed with cunning *coffrets*, petite pastel *macarons* and tempting trays of truffles. In the States we call this, rather prosaically, "Window shopping." In France, they call it "lèche-vitrine." Licking the windows.

"Food porn!" I labeled the photos I sent Marc. He was hooked.

"Do you think we could ever do this?" he said wistfully on the phone. The connection sounded as close as if he were calling from across the street, not the Atlantic Ocean.

He has never been to Paris. He has never said this before. I felt a flutter of excitement. *Could we?*

When we were first married, and too poor to travel, I had always assumed that there would be time later, once we'd had children and they were old enough to travel with us. But autism took over our family. Our first son Jonathan was just entering elementary school when his younger brother Mickey was diagnosed. In those early years, the only travel I did was racing with Mickey from occupational therapy to speech therapy to play therapy to therapeutic nursery school and back again. Over the years we've attempted trial — and trying — family trips: a condo on Cape Cod, where Mickey wandered away into the road; or Washington, D.C., where he refused to enter any museums or monuments.

I'm not impulsive (except for agreeing to marry Marc after dating him only two weeks), but I was no sooner off the plane from Paris than I was phoning the travel agent. I made arrangements quickly. Separate flights. Airport transfers. Travel insurance. I knew if we stopped to think too long about it we would talk ourselves out of it.

"Why Paris again?" my neighbor Nancy asked. "Because Marc's never been," I said. But it's more than that. Paris makes me happy. I've been back twice in the past three years. At home, I am the all-consumed mother of a disabled child. In Paris, I become an art and history lover. A *bon vivant*. A *flâneur* — one who saunters. In Paris, I feel young.

We have never left Mickey for a week. He has left us, of course, to go — reluctantly — to a special needs summer program for three weeks. But now he is the one being left. I shudder, thinking how often he asks me, "Do people come back when they die?"

"We'll call him every night," Marc and I keep telling each other. "We'll Skype. Jonathan will spend lots of time with him. We'll make a big calendar the way we do for camp, so Mickey can cross off the days."

"Will it be too much for Milagros?" I worry aloud. She has been his sitter since he was a baby.

"It's time to call in some chips with the neighbors," Marc says.

I think of the bundles of mail and newspapers and packages and dry cleaning we have taken in for vacationing neighbors in the twelve years we have lived here. All the plants we have watered, the fish we have fed, the snowy steps we have shoveled. We are good neighbors. Good sports, too. We've watched everyone else come and go on their Caribbean cruises and their ski trips to Vail and Vermont. Watched and envied and romanticized the flurry of normal family life, even though I know that often family travel is more about balky toddlers and sulky teens than spectacular sunsets and strolling on silken sand.

"What about his meds?" I fret.

"We can set up one of those weekly pill planner trays."

"What if someone drops the tray?"

"We'll set up a back-up tray."

"Like wearing suspenders and a belt?"

"Exactly," he says.

We are covering everything. All the contingencies we can imagine. Maybe even a few we can't. But what of the things we cannot control?

We've revised our wills, but still need to write a Letter of Intent. All the books on special needs planning say it's one of the most important documents a parent can produce. I open one of those books and read, "Imagine if you went away and never came back. Certainly you have a picture of what you would like his life to look like after your death. However, the next caretaker may not have the same ideas and insight as you."

My stomach clenches. "Stop it, "I tell myself sternly. I find myself remembering how when I was small, I loved to listen to my mother read aloud from one of my favorite books, "The Emerald City of Oz." The Wizard takes Dorothy, Aunt Em and Uncle Henry to visit a remote corner of the kingdom called Flutterbudget Center, a town where people worry. Constantly. Obsessively. They begin every statement with "if." When Dorothy hears a woman scream, "Look out or you'll run over my child!" she asks, "Where is your child?" The woman bursts into tears and says, "In the house. But if it should happen to be in the road, and you ran over it, those great wheels would crush my darling to jelly. Oh dear! Oh dear!'" Flutterbudget Center is filled with people who have foolish fears and worries over nothing. They let their nerves and the "what ifs" run away with them.

But are my fears foolish? The seizures are real. The autism is real. The guilt feels real. How dare I be so self indulgent? Trips are frivolous. And costly. We should put that money into the special needs trust instead. And trumping everything: my certainty that no one could possibly love or take as good care of our son as we do.

But don't I count a little? Any therapist would tell me so. Friends are forever saying I should take time for myself. "It's good for him to see he can be fine without you." "Everyone needs to recharge sometimes." "You'll be an even better parent." "It's important for a marriage." But Marc and I already have a strong marriage. As he frequently says, "We're two bodies with one mind."

"Are we really doing this?" we keep saying to each other. Saturday night Marc and I go to dinner at our favorite French bistro. We talk about what we will see and do. "I've been on the web site for the Louvre," he says, excited. "I think I finally understand how it's laid out." "Trust me, you don't," I say, laughing. This is the guy I once saw get lost in Bloomingdale's. As usual, he knows what I'm thinking. "I'd be lost without you," he says.

"That's what GPS is for," I joke. Giddy, we clink our wine glasses. "To Paris," we say.

The next morning I go to get Mickey his meds. I see a little plastic cup on the counter filled with pills. "Did you take them out already?"

"No," Marc says. "Why?"

I look closely. They are the night time meds, not the morning dose. Milagros forgot. She didn't give him his meds last night. The queasy feeling I've been living with since booking the trip blooms into full blown fear. Epilepsy medication needs to be kept at a constant blood level. If that level falls too much, too fast, he could have horrific seizures. We stare at each other.

"How can we do this?" I ask.

Later I relate this to my neighbor Amy. "You're going!" she says flatly. "If I have to come over here every morning and night and make sure he gets the right pills, I will. I'll even sleep here if it makes you feel better. You're going."

The next day, heavy rains close the local parkway. I think, what if there's a Nor'easter while we're away? With tree-toppling winds and flooding? Last winter we lost power for five full days. What if there's an earthquake? The Hudson Valley is full of fault lines. The Kensico Dam might burst. I imagine streams sluicing through the village. Last year a volcanic plume from Iceland shut down all air travel to Europe. My cousins were stranded in Germany. What if I couldn't fly home? I think of planes. Bombs. Terrorism. The Indian Point nuclear reactor is only 20.77

miles away from our house. If it explodes, will Milagros know where to go? I imagine her unable to start the car, fleeing on foot with Mickey and our three cats, then picture the coyotes that have taken to prowling our suburban yards, picking off stray pets and small children.

Someone shake me. *Stop it,* I think. *Just stop it. Breathe.*

Thirty years ago, right after we got engaged, Marc asked my mother, "There's just one thing I have to ask. Is your daughter the kind of person who's only happy when she has something to worry about?"

"Oh yes," my mother said cheerfully. "Are you changing your mind?"

The great regret of my mother's life was that she never travelled to Europe. The reasons were varied and complicated, but I suspect that what underlay all of them was fear. "Each time I go to Florida and say goodbye to your father, it's like a little death," she once confided.

Yes, I think now. Travelling feels like going toe to toe with my own mortality.

But I don't want to look back later on, as my mother did, and regret the roads — or planes, trains and buses — not taken. Somehow I have to put the flutterbudgets on a tighter leash.

I know I'll be dithering until the moment I step on that plane. But I'm choosing to trust that the plans and backstops we are putting in place will be enough. I want to introduce my husband to the place that makes me so happy. We'll picnic in the Bois de Boulogne, and binge on brioches from the best boulangerie on the Rue de Bac. I want to wander those wondrous streets together, and watch him fall in love with Paris too. We are going to *lèchons* those *vitrines*. Together.

Robert Day
CHANCE ENCOUNTERS OF A LITERARY KIND: MAVIS GALLANT (1922-2014)

It was through Phyllis Springer and Goksin Sipahioglu, the owners of the celebrated photo agency SIPA press in Paris, that I met Mavis Gallant. This was in the 1980s.

Mavis lived in the apartment next to Phyllis and Goksin on the left bank near Boulevard Montparnasse, not far from 27 rue de Fleurus. In that same apartment building in those days lived the Czech novelist Milan Kundera, with whom I had no encounter.

I had been staying in Paris above a couscous restaurant on rue Xavier Privas that I shared with fullback-sized cockroaches. In those days I drove a yellow *deux chevaux* I named Colette. I would park her where I could, changing places in a failed attempt to avoid parking tickets, but at least not being towed.

Some days I'd buy a lunch from *un marchand de rue* and, with a bottle of *vin de pays*, take my meal on Square du Vert Galant, a point on l'Ile de la Cité where I'd watch the *bateaux mouches* on the Seine. One such lunch I saw a barge going up the river packed with cars; Colette was among them — in fact, on the bow, like a figurehead.

It took three days of my poor French and 300 Francs to free her from the *fourrière*, a kind of dog pound for cars. Later, just before I left Paris, I put an AV sign in the windshield and sold her to a *sous chef* of Café de Palais on Place Dauphine. *Adieu*: Colette.

Sometimes Phyllis and Goksin would invite me to join them for dinner at a restaurant where they were habitués. It was at one of those meals that I met Mavis: La Marlotte? Brasserie Lipp? Closerie des Lilas?

Probably La Marlotte, as that was not far from where they all lived.

It was at that meal that Christiane Amanpour stopped to say hello to Gokskin and Phyllis; she had worked for them at SIPA before she turned to television reporting.

— He is a great photographer, she said to me, putting her hand on Gokskin's shoulder. Do you know that? I said I did. And Mavis is a great writer, she continued. I said I knew that as well.

I had, like almost any American author who writes short fiction, read Mavis's stories in the *New Yorker*. Along with Salinger and John Cheever in those days, you could earn multiple graduate degrees in creative writing by reading these authors. At one point I typed (on a manual typewriter, it was that long ago) parts of stories from all three to see what they had accomplished, and how they did it. I learned, among other things, what a fine sense of local detail these writers had: Salinger for the parks and subways of New York City; Cheever for the upstate suburbs with roaming lovers and Labrador Retrievers; Mavis Gallant for the rues of Paris; her stories were their own *plans de Paris*.

Also at that first dinner, Phyllis asked Mavis if she had walked that day. Paris has many rainy days, and that had been one of them.

— I walk every day in Paris, Mavis said. It is how I fetch my stories. Not to do so would be impossible.

Years later, when she was crippled by arthritis and diabetes, Mavis's agent made her a Christmas gift: a year's worth of taxi rides so she could continue fetching her stories.

I imagine her with the notebook of her writer's mind open through her eyes as she has the driver take her toward Place de l'Odéon, and then down where the students rioted in 1968. The next day the taxi is driving her across the Seine toward the Hôtel de Ville in the 4th, past the apartment buildings and cafes and art galleries of her characters, and beyond: to Père Lachaise in the 20th — all the time Mavis not looking where she had been in her previous work, but where in her mind's eye she would be setting new stories once she got back to her writing.

In the years that followed our first dinner, Mavis and I would eat entre nous at restaurants that her characters and mine frequented; she would order from my fictional menu, and I would order from hers —

both being true to our characters. Because of the writer she was, and because of the writer I was, her characters were much better fed than mine. *Tant pis.* At least I ate well, and in her company had bright and witty talk.

At one such lunch (at Le Cherche Midi I think because it was open on Sunday), she lectured me that I was not a writer because I did not make my living as one; beyond that, I taught creative writing, which is not how writers learn. I said I knew the latter from reading her stories. She smiled.

As if to compensate for her rather pointed points, she ordered a split of Château D'ay (the appellation delighted her given the company), and toasted the quality of my fiction: Très amusant, which was high praise, as she thought herself a comic writer.

Très belle:

To Mavis Gallant, after all these years I toast both the woman and her fiction, as if the two can be separated which, had you watched her walking through Paris in the rain (as I did one day on my way to join her for lunch, her head turned here and there to see what would become the facts of her fiction) you know is, thankfully, impossible.

Bobbi Lurie
I HOLD MY BOL OF CAFÉ AU LAIT IN BOTH HANDS

I force myself to focus on the ochre tablecloth, splattered with shadows from the vase of Gourdon flowers. A sense of life's brevity fills me. I want to be mesmerized by light and shadow but my mind wanders. I need to somehow feel I am home; I need a place to call my own. Living in Paris was always my dream. And I have made it come to pass. I turn slightly to my left and see the clock tower of the Church of *Saint Michel des Batignolles* from the kitchen window.

I know I am lucky to have a flat in the 17th arrondisement.

The balcony is too narrow to stand on it. Still, every morning, I open the stained, velvet curtains, pull the shutters back, allow my face to feel the crisp air of *la France*. I hold my bol of café au lait in both hands. I dip a stale piece of yesterday's baguette into the bol. Later, perhaps, I'll buy a croissant, with a demitasse of stronger brew. *Lately, all I eat or drink is coffee and bread.*

It's mid-morning and I must decide whether or not to use my limited energy to walk downstairs to the *Village Café* where they give us blankets when it's cold. I love that place but walking downstairs means having to walk back up. I must plan my day around this fact. I drink from the bol, using the baguette to soak up the last drop of coffee.

I ran away after the clinic shut down. *I lost access to the experimental treatment. I left after the scans came back; I left in the middle of the night. I didn't want to go through surgery again. Or chemo.* I figured everyone would be fine without me. I left my final will and testament, a single hand written Post-it note, next to Nathan's keys. I left my life, thanks to money I saved surreptitiously, while working as a therapist; it's money I put away in increments, in envelopes; money earned through my ability to listen. *But now I desperately need time alone, time with myself, the person who comforts others.*

I walk away from the window, step into the darkened apartment: everything utilitarian, at best. This flat was given to me, no questions asked. And I, in return, ask no questions. Whoever lived here before me hasn't emptied a single drawer of torn underwear or newspaper clippings in a language I cannot decipher; the closet is crammed tight with black dresses. I avoid touching anything.

I fold my clothes on the torn, plastic sofa; I stack my books in the corner. I keep my make-up and medicines in a bag on the kitchen table. My minimal needs and demands make me feel as if I'm entering life as a twenty year old, not leaving it at forty five. I don't care if I barely have enough space for my meager possessions. *This must be home. My last stop.*

•

Un croissant, s'il vous plait, I say, later, in the boulangerie downstairs, using the formal *vous*, even though I've ordered a croissant from her almost every day of the week for the past six months. *Et une demitasse, s'il vous plait*, I add, with a smile, wondering if the powder and blush on my face has managed to cover the state of my health, *my yellow skin*. Her eyes mirror nothing back.

I sit in the corner by the window, looking out at the gray day, eating my croissant, savoring my demitasse.

I need to take the metro. I dread the sharp descent leading down to the trains; I dread being surrounded by my fellow man; man from every race, from every place on earth.

I took on part time work, provided by a man I met on the plane on the way over. I explained myself to him and he seemed to understand. Perhaps it was the language barrier, or the way strangers are easier to speak to. He was from some Middle Eastern country. I often wonder which country he's from. I never asked. I just remember him reading The Koran, whispering each sentence, like a furtive message. I tried not to listen when he spoke about the martyrs. I thought of 9/11 and all the dead; the searching for bodies after, for body parts, for DNA; the superficiality of congeniality, and my fear of revealing my true feelings, felt useless and frightening; still, I took the job.

Yes, I said, when he offered, I can do that. I can pick up your daughter up after her school lets out. I never had kids of my own.

He told me I could use one of his flats. Zis lady is in Germany for all ze time now. Ya can haff za place. I give ta ya za key, he said as a question and answer, both, taking a key out of a pocket from his black, leather jacket, and I write down zee place of it. He wrote the address in the notebook I use to keep track of my symptoms. Here, ya call ma ya need ta at zee headquarters. He handed me his card. On zee back ya see za cell phone of me.

•

The air in Paris was as polluted as it is in Missouri, the people dressed in polyester, just like back home. The old women were as stooped and alone as they were in Kansas City. Pity is the human condition. *Pitiful is what we seek to prevent.*

Dr. Lehman gave me a due date for death. I decided I would stay in Paris and await it. I would give up the idea of loved ones, or friends, who no longer felt like friends, who told me to think positive or stopped speaking to me altogether after I explained my situation. I only wanted my solitude; I only wanted to savor the one thing I avoided all my life, the fact that any possible trust must be resting inside myself.

•

Bonjour Madame, said Farideh when I picked her up at her school, where the teachers treated children like precious cargo, simultaneously doling out a strictness forbidden in America.

I would walk her to Timgad on rue Brunel, as always. We would wait for one of the many men who came to get her.

Bonjour ma petite, I had learned how to say a few things in French. I had also learned to wear scarves, to never leave the apartment without makeup; to wake up to my coffee, ma bol of steaming coffee, mixed with hot milk, standing at the window, leaning towards the balcony... *the view.*

EDITOR

Jessie Vail Aufiery is the World Literature Editor at *The Literary Review*. Find her online at jessievailaufiery.com.

CONTRIBUTORS

Renée Ashley's most recent book of poems is *Because I Am the Shore I Want to Be the Sea*. Her new collection, *The View from the Body*, will be published by Black Lawrence Press in Spring 2016. She teaches in the low-residency MFA in Creative Writing at Fairleigh Dickinson University.

Bettina Ballard (1905-1961) was an editor of *Vogue*. After working for the fashion magazine in New York, she became a Voguette in Paris during the years between the wars before returning to New York.

Wendy Barnes' poems have appeared in publications like *Painted Bride Quarterly*, *Spiral Orb*, *Podium*, *Section 8*, *No, Dear,* and *Slice Magazine*. Her chapbook, *So-Called Mettle*, was published in 2012 (Finishing Line Press). She is a doctoral candidate in the Arts and Letters Program at Drew University. She lives in Brooklyn.

Laure-Anne Bosselaar is the author of *The Hour Between Dog and Wolf*, of *Small Gods of Grief*, which won the *Isabella Gardner Prize for Poetry,* and of *A New Hunger* selected as an *ALA Notable Book for 2008*. With her husband Kurt Brown, she translated a book by Flemish poet, Herman de Coninck: *The Plural of Happiness*. The editor of four anthologies, and the recipient of a Pushcart Prize, she taught at Emerson College, Sarah Lawrence College, and is part of the core faculty at the Low Residency MFA in Creative Writing Program of Pine Manor College.

Christopher Buckley's *Star Journal: Selected Poems* is published by the University of Pittsburgh Press, 2016. Third nonfiction book, *Holy Days of Obligation*, Lynx House Press, 2014. Editor *On The Poetry of Philip Levine:*

Stranger to Nothing. "Our Own Philip Levine" essay in memoriam in June 2015 issue of *Five Points.* Recipient of a Guggenheim in Poetry, two NEAs, Fulbright Award in Creative Writing, four Pushcart Prizes; 2013 winner of the Campbell Corner Poetry Contest.

Liane Kupferberg Carter is the author of the memoir *Ketchup is my Favorite Vegetable: A Family Grows Up With Autism* (Jessica Kingsley Publishers), from which this essay is excerpted. Her work has appeared in the *New York Times,* the *Chicago Tribune, Brevity, Literary Mama, The Manifest-Station,* and many other publications. For more information, visit her website: www.lianekcarter.com.

Allison M. Charette translates literature from French into English. She received a 2015 PEN/Heim Translation Fund Grant for *Beyond the Rice Fields* by Naivo, the first novel to be translated from Madagascar. She founded the Emerging Literary Translators' Network in America (ELTNA. org), a networking and support group for early-career translators. Allison has published two book-length translations, in addition to short translated fiction that has appeared in The Other Stories, InTranslation, the SAND Journal, and others. Find her online at charettetranslations.com.

Jean-Paul Clébert (1926-2011) is the author of more than forty works of fiction and nonfiction. He left Jesuit school at 16, to join the French Resistance, and afterward, traveled Asia. In the 1950s, he frequented two related movements— dwindling Surrealism and burgeoning Situationism — as well as reporting from Asia for *Paris Match* and *France Soir.* The 1996 *Dictionnaire du surréalisme,* for which he single-handedly composed every entry, is widely considered a classic, as is his first book, *Paris insolite* [Curious Paris], a memoir of homeless life in Paris said to have influenced Henry Miller and the Situationist principle of the *dérive.* Published in 1952 with a dedication to Robert Doisneau and photographs by Patrice Molinard, it was, in the author's own words, "not a story in the journalistic sense, but a personal investigation." Among other prominent works are *The Blockhouse* (1958), his only translated novel, and 1962's *Les Tziganes,* a pioneering sociological study of Gypsies also based on personal experience, translated into English by Charles Duff (Dutton, 1963). His later works were dedicated to the history, nature, and culture of Provence, where he spent his final years.

Barbara Crooker is the author of six books of poetry; *Barbara Crooker: Selected Poems* is the most recent. She has received a number of awards, including the 2004 WB Yeats Society of New York Award, the 2003 Thomas Merton Poetry of the Sacred Award, and three Pennsylvania Council on the Arts Creative Writing Fellowships. Her work has appeared in a variety of literary journals, including *Common Wealth: Contemporary Poets on Pennsylvania* and *The Bedford Introduction to Literature.* She has received fellowships from the Virginia Center for the Creative Arts; the Moulin à Nef, Auvillar, France; and The Tyrone Guthrie Centre, Annaghmakerrig, Ireland. She has spent time in Paris (but never enough) when her husband worked for Elf Aquitaine as a research chemist.

Walter Cummins' seventh short story collection, *Telling Stories: Old & New*, was published in 2015. He teaches in the low-residency MFA in Creative Writing at Fairleigh Dickinson University.

Robert Day is the author of eight books, including novels, short fiction, poetry, literary non-fiction, and memoir. More recent are *Chance Encounters of the Literary Kind* (memoir: Serving House Books); *The Billion Dollar Dream* (short fiction: Bookmark); *Let Us Imagine Lost Love* (a novel: Thane and Prose); and *Robert Day for President* (autobiography: Chester River Press).

Gregg Ellis teaches at the University of Toulouse 1, Capitole. Other translations of Philippe Soupault's work have appeared in *Poetry East, Onthebus,* and *The PN Review.*

Edward Gauvin has received fellowships and residencies from PEN America, the NEA, the Fulbright program, the Lannan Foundation, and the French Embassy. His work has won the John Dryden Translation prize and the Science Fiction & Fantasy Translation Award, and been nominated for the French-American Foundation and Oxford Weidenfeld Translation

Prizes. Other publications have appeared in *The New York Times*, *Tin House*, *Harper's*, and *World Literature Today*. The translator of more than 200 graphic novels, he is a contributing editor for comics at *Words Without Borders*.

Kathleen Graber is the author of two collections of poetry, including *The Eternal City*, which was a finalist for The National Book Award, The National Book Critics Circle Award, and the winner of The Library of Virginia Literary Award for Poetry. Recent poems have appeared in *Best American Poetry (2012, 2014)* and *The Pushcart Anthology*. She is the Director of the MFA Program in Creative Writing at Virginia Commonwealth University.

Julien Green (1900-1998) was born to American parents in Paris, and a novelist primarily known for his simple, austere style and his diaries, which were published in nineteen volumes and span the years 1919 to 1998, providing a chronicle of his literary and religious life, and a unique window on the artistic and literary scene in Paris. His themes included faith, religion, hypocrisy, and homosexuality. He wrote primarily in French and was the first non-French national to be elected to the Académie française. A descendant on his mother's side of a Confederate Senator, he self-identified as a Southern writer and wrote several novels in that gothic, nostalgic tradition. Despite also writing in English, and even translating some of his own works with his sister, he remains far better known in France than in Anglophone countries.

Jeanie Greensfelder is the author of *Biting the Apple* (Penciled In, 2012), and *Marriage and Other Leaps of Faith* (Penciled In, 2015). Her poems have been published at *Writer's Almanac* and *American Life in Poetry*; in anthologies: *Pushing the Envelope: Epistolary Poems*, and *30 Years of Corner of the Mouth*; and in journals: *Askew, Miramar, Orbis, Kaleidoscope, Riptide, Falling Star, If&When* and others. She won the Lillian Dean Poetry Award, 2013.

Alison Jarvis's work has appeared in many journals including: *Chelsea, Cream City Review, Gulf Coast, Notre Dame Review, Seattle Review,* and *upstreet.*

She is a recipient of the Lyric Poetry Prize from the Poetry Society of America, the Mudfish Poetry Prize, a Pushcart nomination, and a fellowship from the MacDowell Colony. *Listen* received the Guy Owen Prize from *Southern Poetry Review.*

Ethan Joella teaches English and psychology at University of Delaware and runs his own business that specializes in writing workshops and online instruction. He is editor-at-large at *Referential*. Additionally, his work has appeared in *Best New Writing 2008, The International Fiction Review, The MacGuffin, Rattle, Delaware Beach Life,* and *The Delmarva Review.*

Thomas E. Kennedy's more than 30 books include most recently the novels of the Copenhagen Quartet: *In the Company of Angels* (2010), *Falling Sideways* (2011), *Kerrigan in Copenhagen* (2013), and *Beneath the Neon Egg* (2014), all from Bloomsbury. His stories, essays, and translations have appeared in many journals, including *The Southern Review, New Letters, Epoch, the New Yorker on-line, Esquire Weekly, American Poetry Review, The Literary Review,* and many others. His writing has won a National Magazine Award, two Pushcart Prizes, an O. Henry Award, a Charles Angoff Award, and other prizes. He teaches in the Fairleigh Dickinson University MFA Program.

Philip Kobylarz is a teacher and writer of fiction, poetry, book reviews, and essays. He has worked as a journalist and film critic for newspapers in Memphis, TN. His work appears in such publications as *Paris Review, Poetry,* and *The Best American Poetry* series. The author of a book of poems concerning life in the south of France, he has recently published a short story collection titled *Now Leaving Nowheresville.*

Andrei Konchalovsky was born in 1937 into one of Russia's most famous families. As a film student he collaborated on groundbreaking screenplays with budding legend Andrei Tarkovsky before cementing his own place in Soviet cinema, then leaving Moscow at no small scandal for Hollywood – where he hawked caviar to make ends meet while trying to remake a career, all the while dogged by rumors that he was a KGB agent. Eventually he would leave his mark in Hollywood, too, making films with actors ranging from Jon Voight to Sylvester Stallone, and Barbara Hershey to Whoopi Goldberg. In the 1990s he returned to Russia, continuing to direct movies, plays and operas. In 2014 he was named best director for *The Postman's White Nights* at the Venice International Film Festival.

Scott Lambridis' debut novel, *The Many Raymond Days*, about a scientist who discovers the end of time, received the 2012 Dana Award and is represented by Richard Florest of Robert Weisbach Creative Management. Stories of his have appeared in Amazon's *Day One, Slice, Memorious, Cafe Irreal, Painted Bride*, and other journals. He recently completed his MFA from San Francisco State where he received the Miriam Ylvisaker Fellowship and three literary awards. Before that, he earned a degree in neurobiology, and co-founded Omnibucket.com, through which he co-hosts the Action Fiction! performance series.

Heather Lang is a poet, literary critic, essayist, and adjunct professor. Her poetry has been published by or is forthcoming in *Pleiades, The Normal School*, and *Whiskey Island* among other publications. Her chapbook manuscript was named a semifinalist in the 2014 Tupelo Press Snowbound Chapbook competition, her poetry has been twice nominated for Pushcart Prizes, and she was awarded the Spain 2015 Murphy Writing scholarship. Heather, a Fairleigh Dickinson University MFA graduate, is an editor for *The Literary Review* and *Petite Hound Press*, and she will serve as an AWP16 moderator/panelist. Her website is www.heatherlangwrites. com.

Bobbi Lurie is the author of four poetry collections, most recently, "the morphine poems." (Otoliths)(Austrailia) Her poems can be found in *Fence, New American Writing, APR*, and *Vol.1 Brooklyn*. The beginning chapters of her book on Marcel Duchamp can be found in *Berfrois*.

Bryon MacWilliams is an American writer and translator whose memoir, *With Light Steam: A Personal Journey through the Russian Baths*, was published in October 2014 by NIU Press. He won awards for his reporting at U.S. daily newspapers before moving in the mid-90s to Moscow, where he was based for nearly twelve years as a foreign correspondent covering the territories of the former Soviet Union. He has written for numerous publications big and small, including: *The New York Times*, *The Chronicle of Higher Education*, *Nature*, *Science*, *The Philadelphia Inquirer*, and *The Literary Review*.

Debra Marquart is a professor of English in the MFA Program in Creative Writing & Environment at Iowa State University and the senior editor of *Flyway: Journal of Writing and Environment*. She also teaches in the Stonecoast Low-Residency MFA Program at the University of Southern Maine. Marquart is the author of five books, including three poetry collections—*Small Buried Things, Everything's a Verb,* and *From Sweetness*—and a short story collection, *The Hunger Bone: Rock & Roll Stories*, which draws on her experiences as a female road musician. Marquart's memoir, *The Horizontal World: Growing up Wild in the Middle of Nowhere*, received the "Elle Lettres" award from *Elle Magazine* and the 2007 PEN USA Creative Nonfiction Award. Marquart is currently at work on a nonfiction book, "Schizophonia: Notes on a Life in Music," which is an acoustic ecology on the art of listening, an autobiography of dreaming and catastrophe, and a meditation on the pleasures of making and performing music.

Laura McCullough's most recent book, of poems, *Jersey Mercy*, is forthcoming in 2016 from Black Lawrence Press. Her other books include, *Rigger Death & Hoist Another* (BLP), PANIC (Alice James Books), and *Speech Acts* (BLP), and she is the editor of two anthologies, *A Sense of Regard: Essays on Poetry and Race* (Georgia University Press) and *The Room and the World: Essays on Stephen Dunn* (University of Syracuse Press). Visit her at www.lauramccullough.org.

Josip Novakovich teaches at Concordia in Montreal. His latest book is *Ex-YU*. He has won an Ingram Merrill Award, American Book Award, and a Whiting.

Anne Britting Oleson lives and writes from side of a mountain in central Maine. Her chapbooks are *The Church of St. Materiana* (Moon Pie Press, 2007) and *The Beauty of It* (Sheltering Pines Press, 2010); two other chapbooks, *Trains, Planes and Automobiles* (Portent Press) and *Counting the Days* (Pink Girl Ink) are forthcoming, and a novel, *The Book of the Mandolin Player* (Bedazzled Ink) will be published in 2016.

David Radavich's recent poetry collections are *America Bound: An Epic for Our Time* (2007), *Canonicals: Love's Hours* (2009), and *Middle-East Mezze* (2011). His plays have been performed across the U.S., including six Off-Off-Broadway, and in Europe. He has served as president of the Thomas Wolfe Society and Charlotte Writers' Club and is currently president of the North Carolina Poetry Society. His latest book is *The Countries We Live In* (2014). www.davidradavich.org.

Michèle Rakotoson is one of the most successful and critically-acclaimed authors in Madagascar. The author of numerous prizewinning novels, short stories, and plays, she began her writing career in France for political reasons, but now publishes her work exclusively with Malagasy houses. In 2012, the Académie française awarded her the Grande Médaille de la francophonie for her body of work. Her short stories have appeared in English translation in *From Africa*, as well as the bilingual *Voices from Madagascar*. In addition to writing, she focuses most of her time on championing the next generation of Malagasy writers, by organizing readings, salons, and conferences in Madagascar.

Tegan Raleigh is a PhD candidate in Comparative Literature at UC Santa Barbara. She received her BA in French Literature from Reed College and an MFA in Literary Translation from the University of Iowa. She has translated numerous works of both fiction and non-fiction from French and German and has been the recipient of the PEN translation fund grant and a fellowship from the American Literary Translators Association. In addition, she has been a translator-in-residence at the Banff Literary Centre in Canada and the College des Traducteurs Littéraires in Arles, France. She is currently a lecturer at l'Université de Paris-8 in Saint-Denis.

Lauren Rusk teaches at Stanford University, including its programs in

Paris, Oxford, and Berlin, and has also taught at Swarthmore College and the A Room of Her Own Foundation's retreat. Her books are the poetry collection *Pictures in the Firestorm* (revised second edition, 2015) and a study of autobiographical prose, *The Life Writing of Otherness: Woolf, Baldwin, Kingston, and Winterson* (2002, 2009). Rusk's poems and essays have appeared in such publications as *Hotel Amerika, the Writer's Chronicle*, and *Best New Poets*, whose Open Competition Prize she won.

Thaddeus Rutkowski is the author of the books *Violent Outbursts, Haywire, Tetched* and *Roughhouse*. He received a fellowship in fiction writing from the New York Foundation for the Arts. His stories have appeared in *The New York Times,* the *International Herald Tribune* and many other publications. He lives in Manhattan with his wife and daughter.

Carly Sachs received her MFA in Poetry from The New School. Her poetry has been included in The Best American Poetry 2004 and her fiction has been read on NPR. She is the author of *the steam sequence* and the editor of the anthology, *the why and later*. She has been a teaching artist with The Community Word Project in New York City and with the Wick Poetry Center in Kent, Ohio. Currently, she is leading Yoga Teacher Training at One Love Yoga in Kent, Ohio.

Peter Selgin's *Drowning Lessons* won the 2007 Flannery O'Connor Award for Fiction. He has written a novel and two books on the craft of writing, as well as plays and children's books. His essay collection, *Confessions of a Left-Handed Man*, was short-listed for the William Saroyan International Prize. His memoir, *The Inventors*, is forthcoming from Hawthorne Books in April 2016. He teaches at Antioch University's graduate writing program and is Assistant Professor of English at Georgia College & State University.

Philippe Soupault was born in 1897 and died in 1990. He was a French poet, novelist, essayist, playwright, art reviewer, editor, and also wrote programs for radio. His bibliography includes over 75 titles. The majority of his work, however, is not very well known as he is most often cited as one of the early Surrealists and the co-author of *The Magnetic Fields* with André Breton. He continued to write poems until the end of his life and "Bells of Paris," included in this selection, is an uncollected poem from late in his life. "Westwego" was written from 1917 to 1922 and "Hands That Pray" was published in 1926.

Gladys Swan has published three novels, *Carnival for the Gods* (Vintage Contemporaries Series), *Ghost Dance:A Play of Voices* (LSU Press, nominated for the PEN/Faulkner Award), and *A Dark Gamble*, the first novel of a trilogy set in New Mexcio, as well as seven collections of short fiction. Her poetry, essays, and short stories have appeared in many literary magazines and anthologies. She was just awarded the Andrew Lytle Prize for the best short story published in the *Sewanee Review* in 2015. Though she has spent most of her career as a writer, she has devoted much of the last two decades to painting and exploring the creative process. She was the first writer since the inception of the Vermont Studio Center to receive a fellowship for a residency in painting. Her New Mexico trilogy is being published by Serving House Books. *The Carnival Quintet*, the outgrowth of her first novel, is forthcoming from Kiwai Media in Paris.

Anne Harding Woodworth is the author of five books of poetry and three chapbooks, with a fourth, *The Last Gun*, coming out in 2016. Her poetry, essays, and reviews appear in literary journals in the U.S. and abroad, as well as on line. Her series of persona poems, "Hannah Alive," has morphed into a one-woman play, which had a reading in Washington, D.C. by acclaimed actor Kimberly Schraf.

PARIS ILLUSTRATIONS

TUBIDU GRAPHICS

Brigitta Racz

Established in 2011 in Paris, France, Tubidu Graphics is a graphic design and illustration studio, currently located in Germany. The founder, Brigitta Racz, graduated in as an architect from the University of West Hungary in 2005 and spent a few years working as an interior designer in Budapest and in Paris. Tubidu Graphics was born in 2011 with the idea to combine the artist's background in architecture with her passion for drawing and art. Her latest works of art are renowned for their colorful illustrations focusing on Paris.

CREDITS

Jessie Vail Aufiery, "Diabolo Menthe" first published in *The Writing Disorder*

Bettina Ballard, "The Rebirth of Paris" from Bettina Ballard, *In My Fashion*

Wendy Barnes, "The Flâneuse, or Woman Pendue" and "Men to Ruin, Men to Death" first published in *So-Called Mettle* (Finishing Line Press, 2012).

Christopher Buckley, "The Arborigines in the Jardin des Plantes," "On the Eiffel Tower," and "Photograph of Myself by Modigliani's Grave, Pere Lachaise, 1984" first published in *Blue Autumn* (Copper Beech Press, 1990). "Paris Dispatch" first published in *Sky* (Sheep Meadow Press, 2004).

Liane Kupferberg Carter, "Licking the Windows" first published in *Ketchup is my Favorite Vegetable: A Family Grows Up With Autism* (Jessica Kingsley Publishers).

Jean-Paul Clébert, "The Bawdyhouse for Beggars" — Translated by Edward Gauvin from Chapter 5 of *Curious Paris* (1952 Éditions Denoël, reprinted 1981 and 2009, Éditions Attila).

Barbara Crooker, "Vol De Nuit/ Night Flight" first published in *Americans in Paris* and in *Line Dance* (Word Press, 2008); "In Paris" first published in *The MacGuffin* and in *Radiance* (Word Press, 2005); "Arabesque" first published in *The Writer* and in *Line Dance* (Word Press, 2008); "Nocturne in Blue" first published in *New Millennium Writings* and in *Radiance* (Word Press, 2005); "At the Cimitiere de Montmartre" first published in *Piedmont Literary Review* and in *Barbara Crooker: Selected Poems* (FutureCycle Press, 2015).

Walter Cummins, "The Beauties of Paris" first published *Best New Writing 2007* and in *The End of the Circle* (Hopewell Publications, 2010).

Jeanie Greensfelder, "A Champs-Élysées Stroll 1980" first published in *Biting the Apple* (Penciled In, 2012) and in *Marriage and Other Leaps of Faith* (Penciled In, 2015).

Thomas E. Kennedy, "You Don't Remember Me, But I Remember You," first published in *Serving House Journal*.

Bobbi Lurie, "I hold my bol of café au lait in both hands" first published in *Vol. 1, Brooklyn*, March, 2014.

Laura McCullough, "The Elisionist" first published in *Speech Acts*, Black Lawrence Press.

David Radavich, "Every Day the World Starts Again" first published in *The Countries We Live In* (2014); "Wolfe in Paris" first published in the *Thomas Wolfe Review* (2009).

Michèle Rakotoson, "She, In Springtime" — Translated by Allison M. Charette first published in *Elle, au printemps* (1996, Éditions Sépia).

Lauren Rusk, "Adrift at Notre Dame" first published in *Best New Poets* (Samovar Press/Meridian, 2005).

Thaddeus Rutkowski, "Pardon My French" first published in *Sensitive Skin* magazine

Gladys Swan, "The Turkish March" first published in *Writer's Forum* and *Paraspheres: Fabulist and New Wave Fabulist Fiction;* reprinted in *The Tiger's Eye: New & Selected Stories* (Serving House Books, 2011).

Anne Harding Woodworth, "André Kertész, Photographer" and "Papillon di Seta Blu" first published in *Unattached Male* (Poetry Salzburg, April 2014).

ACKNOWLEDGMENTS

Many thanks to Walter Cummins and Thomas E. Kennedy for creating Serving House Books, and for inviting me to edit this anthology. (Thanks, too, to Walter for his invaluable advice during this process, and for his generosity and hard work, always.)

Thanks to Renée Ashley, Letisia Cruz, Becky Fine-Firesheets, Heather Lang, Minna Proctor, René Steinke, and Jen Werner for their support in matters literary and beyond.

A big thanks to Cristina Favretto at University of Miami Special Collections for her love and knowledge of all things Paris, and for lending me a copy of Bettina Ballard's currently out of print *In My Fashion*. Thanks, too, to the family of Bettina Ballard—Robert F.R. Ballard, Bettina Lindsay Jenney, and Seton Lindsay O'Reilly—for kindly allowing me to print a chapter from that fascinating book.

Finally, I'd like to express my gratitude to Carol VanderStraeten, whose donation of $1000 allowed me to include translations that would not otherwise appear in these pages.

www.ingramcontent.com/pod-product-compliance
Lightning Source LLC
Chambersburg PA
CBHW02055418180626
46810CB00007B/2496